W9-AXF-765

Mary Shelley's
MONSTER

THE STORY OF
FRANKENSTEIN

Mary Shelley's

MONSTER

Martin Tropp

Illustrated with photographs

Houghton Mifflin Company Boston

1976

Library of Congress Cataloging in Publication Data
Tropp, Martin. Mary Shelley's monster.
Filmography: p.   Bibliography: p.   Includes index.
1. Shelley, Mary Wollstonecraft Godwin, 1797–1851.
Frankenstein. 2. Shelley, Mary Wollstonecraft
Godwin, 1797–1851 — Characters — Frankenstein.
3. Frankenstein films — History and criticism.
4. Frankenstein films — Chronology. I. Shelley,
Mary Wollstonecraft Godwin, 1797–1851. Frankenstein.
II. Title.
PR5397.F73T7   823'.7   75-44041
ISBN 0-395-24066-2

Printed in the United States of America

W 10 9 8 7 6 5 4 3 2 1

*For my family and friends, and
especially for my daughter,
Elena.*

Acknowledgments

I could never have completed this book alone. Some who helped: Anne Barrett, Burton Cooper, Stephen and Ivy De Rosier, Linda Granfield, Jonathan Galassi, Claire Alfano Hill, Robert Hogan, Joan Reischauer, Jeffrey Smith, John and Annabel Wickersham.

Special thanks to Dan Curtis Productions, Inc., for their script of *Frankenstein* (1973) and to Richard J. Anobile for pictures from his book *Frankenstein*. The book fully re-creates the entire film by means of more than 1000 full-frame blowups and the entire dialogue, and is available in hardcover edition from Universe Books and in softcover edition from Avon Books. U.K. and Commonwealth editions are distributed by Macmillan Ltd., in hardcover, and by Pan Books, Ltd., in softcover.

For her careful editing, many perceptive insights, encouragement, and patience, I thank most of all Sandra Fehl Tropp.

Contents

Prologue : "Hideous Progeny"   I

I : "The Icy Region This Heart Encircles"   11

II : The Waking Dream   19

III : Double Vision   34

IV : From Mind to Machine   52

V : The Monster   66

VI : Re-creation   84

VII : *Frankenstein* Descending   106

VIII : New Blood   122

IX : At the Crossroads   132

Notes   *159*

*A Selected Chronology of
Frankenstein Films*   *169*

A Guide to Further Reading   *175*

Index   *187*

Illustrations

following page 2

Mary Shelley. Portrait by Sir Charles L. Eastlake. (Bodleian Library, Oxford)

Mary Jane (Claire) Clairmont. Portrait by Amelia Curran. (Newstead Abbey, Nottingham Museums)

Villa Diodati. From an engraving by E. Finden after a drawing by W. Purser. (Radio Times Hulton Picture Library)

P. B. Shelley. Portrait by Amelia Curran. (National Portrait Gallery, London)

Lord Byron. Portrait by T. Phillips. (National Portrait Gallery, London)

John W. Polidori. Portrait by F. G. Gainsford. (National Portrait Gallery, London)

Title Page, Mary Shelley's *Frankenstein* (1818). (By permission of the Harvard College Library)

The Nightmare. John Henry Fuseli. (The Detroit Institute of Art, Gift of Mr. and Mrs. Bert L. Smokler and Mr. and Mrs. Lawrence A. Fleischman)

Frankenstein's Castle, Eberstadt, Germany. (Stephen and Ivy DeRosier)

The Fall of the Magician Hermogenes Pave. Pieter Brueghel I, engraved by Petrus a Merica. (The Metropolitan Museum of Art, Harris Brisbane Dick Fund, 1928)

Wild Man Holding Shield with Greyhound. Martin Schongauer. (National Gallery of Art, Washington, D.C., Rosenwald Collection)

The Minotaur. G. F. Watts. (The Tate Gallery, London)

Satan Sowing the Tares. Felicien Rops. (Copyright Bibliothéque royale Albert Ler, Bruxelles, Cabinet des Estampes)

How They Met Themselves. D. G. Rossetti. (Fitzwilliam Museum, Cambridge)

Thomas Potter Cooke as the Monster. Poster painted by Wageman, drawn on stone by N. Whittock. (Harvard Theatre Collection)

Richard John ("O.") Smith as the Monster. (By permission of the Harvard College Library)

Charles Ogle as the Monster. (British Film Institute)

Boris Karloff getting made up as the Monster for *Frankenstein.* (The Museum of Modern Art/Film Stills Archive)

Dwight Frye as Fritz in *Frankenstein.* (Courtesy of Universal Pictures)

Six scenes from *Frankenstein.* (Courtesy of Universal Pictures, and by special arrangement with Darien House, Inc.)

Laboratory Scene from *Frankenstein.* (The Museum of Modern Art/Film Stills Archive and Universal Pictures)

Laboratory Scene from *The Bride of Frankenstein* (The Museum of Modern Art/Film Stills Archive and Universal Pictures)

Boris Karloff on the set of *The Bride of Frankenstein.*

Elsa Lanchester checks her make-up on the set of *The Bride of Frankenstein.* (The Museum of Modern Art/Film Stills Archive and Elsa Lanchester)

The laboratory set for *The Bride of Frankenstein.* (The Museum of Modern Art/Film Stills Archive)

Dr. Pretorious. (The Museum of Modern Art/Film Stills Archive and Universal Pictures)

Dr. Caligari and Cesare. (The Museum of Modern Art/Film Stills Archive)

Dr. Pretorious and the Monster. (Courtesy of Universal Pictures)

Scene from *Son of Frankenstein.* (Courtesy of Universal Pictures)

Boris Karloff as the Monster in *The Bride of Frankenstein.* (Courtesy of Universal Pictures)

Peter Boyle as the Monster in *Young Frankenstein.* © 1974 Twentieth Century-Fox Film Corporation. All rights reserved.

Mary Shelley's
MONSTER

"Hideous Progeny"

What myths are to the race, dreams are to the individual, for in dreams, as in myths, there also appear those primitive emotions and feelings in the form of giants, heros, dragons, serpents, and blood sucking vampires; representations of guilt, retribution, and fate; of lust and power, of monsters of the deep (the unconscious) and of unknown but overwhelming beings which fill our nights with nightmarish dreams and make us fear our sleep, but which, rightly used, can be fruitfully integrated into our personality.

J. A. HADFIELD

MOST OF US first met Frankenstein in the darkness of a movie theater. His story has fascinated film makers and audiences almost from the invention of the medium. Since the first one-reeler in 1910, there have been literally hundreds of versions in many languages, ranging in quality from the James Whale/ Boris Karloff classics to *Jesse James Meets Frankenstein's Daughter* and *Frankenstein De Sade*. Whatever the artistry of the creators, certain elements are constant. There is, of course, a Frankenstein and a Monster — the latter huge, powerful, and misshapen, the former thin, brilliant, and indisputably insane. After appropriate megalomaniacal mutterings, Frankenstein heads for his laboratory, where, in the middle of an electrical display limited only by the size of the budget, he brings the Monster to life. From then on, anything can happen, although most often the result is murder, mayhem, and

I

suitable, if not permanent, destruction of both creation and creator. For a few moments, we may feel pity for the misunderstood and outcast being given life to feed Frankenstein's madness, but the emotion most hoped for and often achieved is a mixture of horror and fascination. The success of the *Frankenstein* formula is proved by the simultaneous popularity of the latest wide-screen, full-color versions and the Universal films from the thirties, which seem to have found eternal life on the television screen. Something about the story is never exhausted, always current, always able to attract a new generation.

Now that movies are studied in universities, the Karloff films have been accorded the deference given "serious" art. But one of the refreshing qualities about *Frankenstein* is that it blurs such distinctions. Whatever is eternal about the tale also appeals to nearly everyone. The Monster has become a cultural mascot. The Living Theatre made it a symbol for oppressed mankind; it has been called the ancestor of "all the shambling horde of modern robots and androids" in science fiction.[1] At the same time, domesticated and dyed purple, it beckons our children to breakfast from a cereal box. Herman Munster, a bumbling and lovable Monster, was for many years the star of a situation comedy. There have been Monster dolls, Monster magazines, Monster T-shirts, "The Monster Mash," and even Monster vitamins. The Monster has been used on television to sell everything from fluorescent lights to automobiles. His creator has spawned a whole range of demented scientists, from Dr. Strangelove to the Saturday morning cartoon madmen whose symptoms include unruly hair, a persistent cackle, and the desire to (dare I say it?) "rule the world!" Mel Brooks' 1974 parody of the tradition, *Young Frankenstein*, is really an affectionate tribute to the story that has become familiar to us all. Mad scientist and Monster are figures in a modern myth; in whatever guise they appear,

Mary Wollstonecraft Godwin Shelley, painted
in the 1830s by Sir Charles L. Eastlake.

Her stepsister and unwanted traveling companion, Mary Jane (Claire) Clairmont, at age 21, painted in 1819 by Amelia Curran.

The Villa Diodati, near Geneva, where, in June of 1816, Mary Shelley listened to the horror stories and scientific speculations that gave her the inspiration for *Frankenstein*.

Shelley, Byron (in Albanian dress), and Polidori. Byron, at 28, was the oldest of the competitors in the ghost story contest. Eight years later, only Mary Shelley was still alive.

FRANKENSTEIN;

OR,

THE MODERN PROMETHEUS.

———

IN THREE VOLUMES.

———

Did I request thee, Maker, from my clay
To mould me man ?   Did I solicit thee
From darkness to promote me ?——
                                    PARADISE LOST.

———

VOL. I.

═══════════

London :

PRINTED FOR
LACKINGTON, HUGHES, HARDING, MAVOR, & JONES,
FINSBURY SQUARE.

———

1818.

The most famous legacy of that summer, *Frankenstein*, was first published anonymously. It gained immediate popularity, despite mixed reviews.

John Henry Fuseli's *The Nightmare*. Fuseli was a friend of the God-
wins; Mary Shelley was quite familiar with this, his most famous
painting. The eyeless horse peering through the bed-curtains resembles
the Monster's appearance at the end of Frankenstein's dream; the
impish creature is an incubus, once believed to cause nightmares by
sitting on the sleeper's chest and exhaling noxious breath in her face.
This is less absurd than it seems, since Ernest Jones describes one of
the features of a nightmare as "sense of oppression or weight at the
chest which alarmingly interferes with respiration."

Frankenstein's Castle, once the site of alchemical experiments, is now little more than a pile of stones, with one suitably spooky tower intact. Lately a hotel and snack bar have been added.

IDEM IMPETRAVIT A DEO VT MAGVS A DEMONIBVS DISCERPERETVR

A version of the Faust myth from the sixteenth century, *The Fall of the Magician Hermogenes Pave*, by Pieter Brueghel I. Although specific references, including the identity of the saint, are obscure, the lesson is vividly depicted. The demons are performing traditional conjuring, acrobatic, and contortionist tricks.

One of the many medieval depictions of the wild
man, *Wild Man Holding Shield with Greyhound*,
by Martin Schongauer.

Opposite:

The Minotaur, like all legendary monsters, stands
outside of the natural order and is therefore opposed to it. In this 1877 painting, G. F. Watts con-
veys the natural order by the Minotaur's oddly
touching expression and the unnatural by what's
under the monster's left hand.

Satan Sowing the Tares by Felicien Rops. A late -
nineteenth-century vision of the urban Lucifer.

The Doppelgänger: *How They Met Themselves*, Dante Gabriel Rossetti's mid-Victorian "autoscopic" fantasy.

Thomas Potter Cooke, the first actor to portray the Monster. The poster does little justice to his make-up, which reportedly gave him a "green and yellow visage, watery and lackluster eye, livid hue of arm and leg, shriveled complexion, lips straight and black, and a horrible ghastly grin."

Richard John O. Smith, who began playing the Monster a few years after Cooke, wore a costume consisting of a "close vest and leggings of pale yellowish brown heightened with blue, Greek shirt of dark brown, and broad black leather belt." This is the frontispiece to H. M. Milner's *Frankenstein, or the Man and the Monster!*, published in 1826.

The EDISON
KINETOGRAM

VOL. 1   LONDON, APRIL 15, 1910   No. 1

SCENE FROM

FRANKENSTEIN

FILM No. 6604

EDISON FILMS TO BE RELEASED FROM MAY 11 TO 18 INCLUSIVE

Charles Ogle, the first movie Monster.

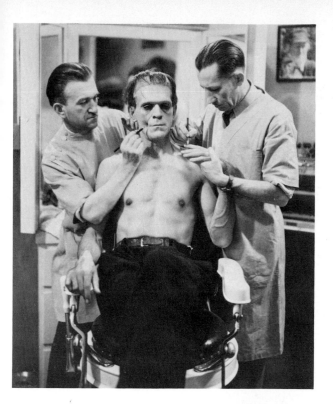

Jack Pierce (l.) and assistant transforming a little-known actor, Boris Karloff, into the definitive twentieth-century incarnation of the Monster.

Dwight Frye as Fritz, the first in a long line of hunchback or otherwise deformed assistants.

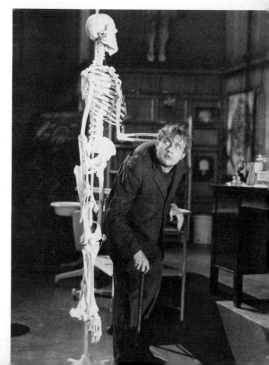

FRANKENSTEIN   In the shadow of Christ and Death, Frankenstein and Fritz prepare to resurrect a body.

Fritz's fire and the sunlight from the window illuminate the Monster.

The only direct "quote" from the novel: "She was there, lifeless and inanimate, thrown across the bed, her head hanging down . . . . her bloodless arms and relaxed form flung by the murderer on its bridal bier . . . The shutters had been thrown back; and . . . I saw at the open window a figure most hideous and abhorred." (Whale hedges a bit; Elizabeth has only fainted.)

Seen through the revolving mill wheel, maker and Monster appear as doubles.

The burning cross. This was originally the last shot in the film.

RENOVATIONS AT THE WATCHTOWER

In this scene from *Frankenstein,* Colin Clive appears to be dissatisfied with the height of his laboratory. Four years later, for the generally baroque *Bride of Frankenstein (opposite),* the roof was raised, and his modest electrical apparatus, pickled salamander, and symbolic lantern were replaced by more elaborate (and appropriately phallic) equipment.

Boris Karloff stops for a smoke between takes.

Elsa Lanchester checks her Monster
make-up.

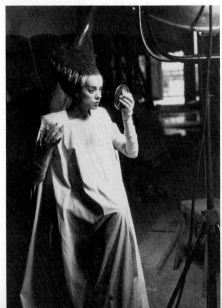

The only identifiable figures on the laboratory set are Dwight Frye in his lab coat and director James Whale (in the center, to the left of the man in the fedora).

Destined to become the spiritual father of Peter Cushing's Baron Frankenstein, Ernest Thesiger's Dr. Pretorious shows his medieval alchemist ancestry as he poses among his homunculi.

FROM CALIGARI TO PRETORIOUS

Caligari's triumphant pose before Cesare's open coffin clearly inspired the scene from *The Bride of Frankenstein*. Caligari holds a stick; Pretorious stands next to a spear. As in the later Hammer films, the creation is only of interest to the doctor because of the power and control it gives him.

Son of Frankenstein first emphasized the scientist as medical doctor and the Monster as lingering patient. Here, the butler and Ygor look on as Basil Rathbone gives the Monster a checkup.

Karloff's performance as the Monster owed as much to what James Whale called his "queer, penetrating personality" as it did to the forty pounds of costume and make-up. Forty years later, in *Young Frankenstein*, Peter Boyle *(overleaf)* was able, despite the zipper and the generally satiric nature of the film, to give his Monster a similar underlying integrity.

they reflect our fears about the future of man in a world of machines.

All of this began one rainy summer night in 1816, with a young woman lying half awake in a Swiss villa on the shores of Lake Leman. Mary Wollstonecraft Godwin was the quietest member of an illustrious circle that included her lover, Shelley, the magnetic Byron, and the slightly mad young doctor John Polidori. The group had been sitting around the fire telling ghost stories; at Byron's suggestion, each tried to think of a tale of his own. Shelley, Byron, and Polidori essentially failed; their productions were eminently forgettable fragments.[2] But Mary Godwin, who had been listening to a discussion of the possibility of giving life to inanimate matter, fused this new horror to the moldy terrors of the Gothic tale. One June night, as she recalled many years later,

> I did not sleep, nor could I be said to think. My imagination, unbidden, possessed and guided me . . . I saw — with shut eyes, but acute mental vision, — I saw the pale student of the unhallowed arts kneeling beside the thing he had put together. I saw the hideous phantasm of a man stretched out, and then, on the working of some powerful engine, show signs of life, and stir with an uneasy, half vital motion. Frightful must it be; for supremely frightful would be the effect of any human endeavour to mock the stupendous mechanism of the Creator of the world. His success would terrify the artist; he would rush away from his odious handy-work, horror-stricken . . . He sleeps; but he is awakened; he opens his eyes; behold the horrid thing stands at his bedside, opening his curtains, and looking on him with yellow, watery, but speculative eyes.
>
> I opened mine in terror. The idea so possessed my mind, that a thrill of fear ran through me, and I wished to exchange the ghastly image of my fancy for the realities around. I see them still; the very room, the dark *parquet*, the closed shutter, with the moonlight struggling through, and the sense I

3

had that the glassy lake and the white high Alps were beyond.
I could not so easily get rid of my hideous phantom; still it
haunted me ... I recurred to my ghost story, — my tiresome
unlucky ghost story! O! if I could only contrive one which
would frighten my reader as I myself had been frightened that night! ... On the morrow I announced that I had
thought of a story. I began that day with the words, *It was a
dreary night of November*, making only a transcript of the
grim terrors of my waking dream.[3]

The essence of the *Frankenstein* myth is contained in this
dream. Twenty-one months of work that resulted in the
publication of *Frankenstein, or the Modern Prometheus* on
March 11, 1818, built upon this vision of blasphemous creation and its hideous results. The dream itself grew out of
the mind of a strange, remarkable woman who could see the
relationship between the potential of man's newfound powers
and the awful destructiveness hidden within the self. In 1831,
Mary Shelley revised, tightened, and considerably improved
her novel for a new edition; she also added an introduction
which tells the story of its origin and ends by bidding her
"hideous progeny go forth and prosper." Even she could
hardly imagine the forms her offspring would take. A Dar-
winian metaphor is apt; *Frankenstein* has become a species, a
product of changes wrought by time and circumstance. The
evolutionary process has come so far that the ancestral novel
has been forgotten by many. An NBC movie that called itself
"The True Story" changed almost every aspect of the plot
and added new characters. Though not the throwback it
claimed to be, this *Frankenstein* was, like all the others, a
reflection of the vision that gave life to the myth. For those
who are unfamiliar with the first *Frankenstein*, the following
few pages briefly summarize the novel. Once we know the
story Mary Shelley finally presented to the world, we can
begin to see why the world took her nightmare for its own.

"Hideous Progeny"

The novel opens in St. Petersburgh late in the eighteenth century. Robert Walton is setting out on a journey of exploration to the North Pole, which he hopes will be an ice-free paradise, "surpassing in wonders and beauty every region hitherto discovered on the habitable globe." [4] His letters to his sister Margaret and the journal he keeps form the body of *Frankenstein*. The first few letters describe his journey and define his past and character. Walton is an isolated, somewhat ruthless individual, who believes "one man's life or death [is] but a small price to pay for the acquisition of the knowledge which I [seek]; for the dominion I should acquire." Although his claim that "there is something at work in my soul, which I do not understand" spurs him on, it is fairly obvious that his explorations compensate for his loneliness; forever lamenting his lack of a true friend, he strives to leave humanity behind and "tread a land never before imprinted by the foot of man." Before his ambition can destroy him, his ship is frozen in the Arctic ice, where he comes across a sledge containing Victor Frankenstein, who has been seen chasing a huge, shadowy figure on another dog sledge. Half-dead with cold and hunger, Frankenstein is brought aboard ship and begins to tell his story.

Now Frankenstein narrates Walton's journal. We learn of his upper-middle-class childhood, his amateur researches into alchemy and the occult, and his journey to the University at Ingolstadt. There, he embarks upon some grisly studies which result in his sudden, miraculous discovery of the power to give life to dead matter. Then comes the core of Mary Shelley's vision: he creates a huge, man-like creature that comes to life and fills its creator with horror and disgust. He runs out of the room and providentially meets his childhood friend, Henry Clerval. Frankenstein decides to keep the Monster's existence a secret since, when they return to his room, the "dreaded spectre" is gone. Yet Frankenstein suddenly imag-

5

ines it "gliding" into the room, falls down in a fit, and spends many months senseless with a "nervous fever." When he recovers, it is only to learn of the murder of his youngest brother, William; he and Clerval return immediately to Geneva. There, he finds out that a young family servant, Justine, has been charged with the murder. Though he glimpses his Monster and somehow knows it is responsible, he does nothing but watch as Justine is sent to the gallows. Retreating into a "deep, dark, deathlike solitude," Frankenstein sets off to climb the glacier at Chamounix where, on Alpine ice fields in the shadow of Mont Blanc, he sees the Monster striding toward him. It leads him to a hut near the summit, where it tells its own story.

The Monster recounts its first, hazy impressions, its painful life alone in a forest near Ingolstadt, and its providential discovery of an isolated family, the De Laceys. From a shack next to their cottage, it secretly spied upon their lives and, incidentally, learned how to read and write French. From some papers in its pocket, the Monster came to know its origins; from the reception mankind gave it, it learned how alone it really was. When the De Laceys also spurned it, the Monster turned against man and nature, burning down the cottage, tearing up the garden, then wandering across the cold landscape until it met a small boy. Through what seems to be an astonishing coincidence, the child was William Frankenstein. The Monster had intended to take him away as a companion; when it discovered his identity, it strangled him with "hellish triumph" and planted the child's locket on the sleeping Justine, thus insuring her conviction for his murder. The Monster ends its story by demanding that Frankenstein create it a mate, promising they will live far from mankind, in the "wilds of South America."

Frankenstein at first consents. He slowly travels up the Rhine and across England followed by his monstrous creation. Finally he sets up his laboratory alone, on an island in the Outer Hebrides, where he puts together his second monster. During a sudden attack of scruples, he destroys his handiwork, infuriating the Monster. Warning him, "I shall be with you on your wedding night," it takes off in a small boat across the Irish Sea and, as we soon learn, promptly strangles Clerval on a beach in Ireland. Frankenstein, who has also set out on a boat in the same direction, washes ashore on the same beach soon after, and is immediately arrested for Clerval's murder. Again he spends two months delirious and near death, but when his father arrives, he is released and sets out for Geneva. Having seemingly forgotten the Monster's warning, he prepares to marry his childhood sweetheart, Elizabeth Lavenza. On his wedding night, true to its word, the Monster strangles Elizabeth — Frankenstein enters his room in time to see it run away and dive into the lake. This time, his delirium is called madness, and Frankenstein spends many months chained in a cell. When he gets out, he travels to the graveyard where the Monster's victims lie and vows to destroy his creation. The response is another glimpse of the creature, again just eluding his grasp. It leads Frankenstein on a long chase across Russia and the Arctic ice, leaving messages and clues to guide him. By the time he arrives at Walton's ship, Frankenstein is dying but still determined to find and put an end to the Monster.

Walton, who doesn't know what to think of this story, is having troubles of his own. His crew refuses to go farther north, despite Frankenstein's exhortation for them to be "more than men." They force Walton to turn around and head back. Although upset by their cowardice, he recognizes that he "cannot lead them unwillingly to danger, and...must return." Frankenstein's final words vacillate between urging Walton onward and telling him to "avoid ambition, even if it be only the apparently innocent one of distinguishing yourself in science and discoveries." After Frankenstein's death, Walton comes upon the Monster, huge and horrible, hanging over its maker's body. It argues that it was "the slave, not the master, of an impulse, which I detested, yet could not disobey." Walton isn't convinced; he condemns the creature as a "hypocritical fiend" who laments the death of Frankenstein "only because the victim of your malignity is withdrawn from your power." The Monster, spurned by the last human it meets, jumps overboard, vowing to immolate itself at the North Pole, and is soon "lost in darkness and distance."

Of course, the Monster wasn't lost for long. Beginning with a play in 1823, there has hardly been a year that the *Frankenstein* story hasn't appeared on stage or screen somewhere in the world. Although none of these versions is faithful to the depth and complexity of the original, most convey the curious combination of dream logic and scientific prophecy that gives the novel its power. Even the common error of calling both the scientist and his nameless creation "Frankenstein" suggests an intuitive knowledge of what this short synopsis hints at — that creator and creature are in some sense two sides of one personality.[5]

Frankenstein is one of those rare works of fiction that is mythopoeic — myth creating. Like Kafka's *The Castle*, it has the timeless feeling of nightmare and a structure that gives form to the experience of living in the modern world. Myth itself is an elastic term, stretched to encompass a wide range of belief, ritual, and literature, while coming to suggest either something patently false or deeply true. *Frankenstein* is mythic in the broadest sense and shares some of the relatively specific elements of anthropological myth as well. Walton's abortive trip to the North Pole is clearly a classic journey of initiation. He meets a superhuman hero and an abominable monster — a half-dead being living in its own Hell. Learning from Frankenstein's failure, and passing the trial of the Monster's nearly persuasive arguments, Walton chooses the path that will lead back to society, having gained new awareness of himself and new knowledge for his culture. The pattern is as old as the *Gilgamesh* epic, *The Divine Comedy*, *Beowulf*, or any other tale that, like *Frankenstein*, has the texture of dream and the vast universe of epic, the cosmic theme of the limits of man and the power of God, and the archetypal motif of a journey. At the same time, Mary Shelley has written a very modern story that defines the relationships between man, machine, and society that arose with the technological revolution.

Much discussion of *Frankenstein* has focused on its relationship to the Romantic movement and the influence of Byron, Shelley, and others on the genesis and shape of Mary Shelley's novel.[6] This book looks at *Frankenstein* as Mary Shelley's independent response to the direction she saw the world taking. By exploring the unusual past and personality of the author as reflected in her novel, we can understand how she used the latest discoveries of science, characters from legend, and the pattern of the epic to transform her private vision into a collective nightmare. Examining some of the films inspired by *Frankenstein* shows us how the basic elements of the story repeat almost ritually, while details change to suit a changing culture. The intent is to understand how the dream of a nineteen-year-old woman could become the myth of technology. Mary Shelley's "waking dream" was more than the inspiration for a novel, it was the visionary moment that brought together many converging forces, the most important point on a path that led from one woman's past to the future of mankind.

CHAPTER I

"The Icy Region This Heart Encircles"

> In summary it may be said that the creative imaginations which
> participate in the formation of a *vital* myth must be those of peo-
> ple — often alienated and withdrawn people — who have *experi-*
> *enced*, in their "depths" and on their own pulses, one or more of
> the unsolved critical situations with which humanity at large or
> members of their own society are confronted.
>
> HENRY A. MURRAY

REALITY NEVER PROVIDED a refuge for Mary Shelley. When
she was ten days old, on September 9, 1797, her mother, the
famous feminist author Mary Wollstonecraft, died from
"childbed sickness." From then on, Mary was barely tolerated
by William Godwin — political philosopher, novelist, perpetual debtor, and Mary's wretched father. His coldness,
cruelty, and intolerance are attested to by virtually anyone
who ever knew or wrote about him. When he married Mary
Jane Clairmont four years later, he brought a stepmother and
stepsiblings into the household. Mary later called Mrs. Clairmont "a woman I shudder to think of." [1] The birth of William
Godwin's namesake further alienated Mary until, as her biog-
raphers agree, she was "driven inward, lonely and self-pitying,
at odds with her companions and her surroundings." [2] A contemporary visitor to the Godwin household described her as a
"sad-eyed little girl who would sit motionless for hours, hardly

daring to breathe." [3] Her few happy times came during a two-year series of trips to relatives in Scotland, far from the oppressive atmosphere of 41 Skinner Street, London. Godwin sent her to Scotland by sea, knowing, as he related in a letter, that "I daresay she will arrive more dead than alive, as she is extremely subject to sea-sickness, and the voyage will, not improbably, last nearly a week." [4] Despite her father's indifference toward her, Mary harbored a "half-obsessive" love for him.[5] The coldness of Godwin's attitude, matched by the unfriendliness of every place outside of her Scottish retreat, helped create the desolation that was Mary Shelley's childhood.

It is little wonder, then, that (as she writes in the 1831 introduction to *Frankenstein*) her fondest childhood memories were of solitary pastimes — reading, writing, and most of all "the formation of castles in the air — the indulging in waking dreams — the following up trains of thought which had for their subject the formation of a succession of imaginary incidents. My dreams . . . were my refuge when annoyed — my dearest pleasure when free." On the "blank and dreary" shores of the Tay, in Scotland, she found a landscape for her fantasies, a place where she could "people the hours with creations far more interesting to me at that age, than my own sensations."

In the spring of 1814, at the age of seventeen, Mary returned from Scotland and met the young poet Shelley, who had come to the household as her father's disciple. In a whirlwind and rather bizarre courtship that included meetings at the grave of her mother, Mary and Shelley became lovers and, on July 28, they ran off together. Yet, in escaping the Godwin household, Mary could not leave her past behind. Her stepsister, Jane (who had renamed herself Claire), came along, and her romantic airs and frequent fits clashed with Mary's bouts of jealousy to keep their relationship tense. Their trip through Europe was something less than a grand tour. Much of the travel was by mule; Mary's journal is full of references to bad food, disagreeable companions, and filthy accommodations. Godwin kept writing them, alternately condemning Mary as a "criminal" and begging them for money. By September they were back in England. The next fourteen months saw Shelley dodging creditors and Mary giving birth to two children — the first, a girl, died after less than two weeks. Finally, in May of 1816, Shelley, Mary, their four-month-old son William, and Claire set off again for Geneva and the rainy summer that spawned *Frankenstein.*

Back in England that fall, Mary Shelley worked on her novel and contended with a host of new and painful problems. On October 9, 1816, Fanny Imlay, Mary's half sister and the member of her household closest to her, poisoned herself with laudanum; on December 15, Shelley's wife, Harriet, drowned herself. Fifteen days later, Shelley and Mary were married. Over twenty years later, Mrs. Shelley's guilt for Harriet's timely death was still strong. She wrote in her journal in 1839, "Poor Harriet, to whose sad fate I attribute so many of my own heavy sorrows, as the atonement claimed by fate for her death." [6] When we add to this the birth of Mary's second daughter, Clara, in late 1817, some months after Claire had a daughter by Byron, as well as the usual battles with her father and Shelley's creditors, one might expect that Mary would be more than a little upset. Yet, throughout this turmoil, she kept her characteristically calm surface; the adjective repeatedly applied to her is "placid."

In fact, she seemed cold to many who knew her. During an even greater period of stress, after Shelley's death, she was described as setting up a "confusing and forbidding barrier of calm and apparent indifference . . . She spoke of Shelley without apparent emotion, without regard, or a feeling approaching regret, without pain as without interest, and seemed to contemplate him, as everything else, through the same passionless medium." [7] Given the setting of *Frankenstein*, told from a ship locked in the Arctic, it is of more than passing interest that Mrs. Shelley's personality was often compared to "ice." Biographer and traveler Edward John Trelawny wrote Shelley, "When us three meet, we shall be able to ice the wine by placing it between us [with Mary]," while actor-playwright John Howard Payne was indelicate enough to ask Mary herself, "Is ice a non-conductor? But, if it is, how do you convey impressions?" [8] This charge, which bothered Mrs. Shelley all her life, resulted from the barrier she set up to protect herself from pain. She wrote in her journal, "Have I a cold heart? God knows! But none need envy the icy region this heart encircles; at least the tears are hot which the emotions of this cold heart forces [*sic*] me to shed." [9] She also wrote, in a letter to Byron, "I am said to have a cold heart — there are feelings however so strongly implanted in my nature that to root them out life will go with it." [10]

The nature of those feelings are suggested by a few slight hints in her guarded journals and letters. During her "elopement," when she was externally happy, she wrote a story with the surprising title "Hate"; it was either destroyed or lost, since only the title is known. She also had fits of brooding and bad temper, directed at Shelley and Claire Clairmont, which distanced her from them both and led to more of her persistent self-examination. In a letter of July 1823, she wrote her son, "... do not let your impatient nature ever overcome you — or you may suffer as I have done — which God forbid! ... remorse is a terrible feeling — and it requires a faith and philosophy immense not to be destroyed by the stinging monster." [11] Thus, in the icy region near her heart lurked strong, lifethreatening feelings that she compared to a stinging monster. The image is paralleled twice in *Frankenstein*. Frankenstein tells Walton, "I ardently hope the gratification of your wishes may not be a serpent to sting you, as mine have been," while the Monster tells Walton, ". . . the bitter sting of remorse will not cease to rankle in my wounds till death shall close them forever."

That Walton hears both statements is significant, since the whole story is obviously intended to teach him where his quest for preeminence actually leads. On a deeper level, the complex "succession of imaginary incidents" that Mary Shelley took nearly two years to spin from her dream was a way for her to examine her attitudes toward herself and those she loved.[12] *Frankenstein* is constructed like a set of Chinese boxes; Walton's letters to his sister Margaret contain Frankenstein's narrative which in turn contains the Monster's story. Each level has its own voice and its own point of view. This layering leads, step by step, through the concentric circles of Mary Shelley's complex personality — past the face she showed to the world and deep into the self she could "hate and despise" [13] to the monster that appeared only in nightmare.

Mrs. Margaret Saville is the outer Mrs. Mary Shelley — the initials provide the first clue. She is mentioned only in the narrative frame, Walton's story, which all evidence shows was written after Mary Shelley's marriage. We learn little about her, except that she is Walton's married sister, removed in space and time from the drama, and that, in Walton's words, "you have a husband, and lovely children; you may be happy." He writes his journal for Margaret, giving his reasons in the question, "What can I say, that will enable you to understand the depth of my sorrow?" He fears that he will never return, his letters will never reach her, and she will be tortured by hope and grief. "And what, Margaret," he asks, "will be the state of your mind?"

We learn more about Robert Walton himself, and what we learn ties him closer to the author. That each of these deeper self-projections is male tells us something about Mrs. Shelley and the society around her. Walton is the self beneath the feminine ("Mrs. Saville") mask of wife and mother, the Mary Shelley often praised for her "masculine" intelligence and understanding. His past mirrors hers. He writes that, during his childhood, "my education was neglected, yet I was passionately fond of reading." At the age of fourteen "I became acquainted with the celebrated poets of our country" and "also became a poet, and for one year lived in a Paradise of my own creation" only to fail and be bitterly disappointed. His favorite poem is Coleridge's *Rime of the Ancient Mariner*, which he sees as reflecting his own interest in traveling to the "land of mist and snow." The young Mary Godwin was similarly "encouraged by her father to educate herself by extensive reading." [14] In 1812, at the age of fourteen, she met Shelley for the first time; in the same year she and her stepsister hid behind a sofa to hear Coleridge himself recite the *Ancient Mariner*. When Mary and Shelley first left for Europe, she brought along a box full of her own youthful poetic efforts; it was left behind in Paris. Although she continued to write poetry, Mary recognized that she could "never write verses except under the influence of a strong sentiment, and seldom even then." [15] (Unfortunately, her published poems bear this out all too well.) Both Walton and Mary desperately wanted true friends yet sought to isolate themselves, spending time in what Walton calls "extended and magnificent" daydreams. Caught in the ice in midjourney, Robert Walton is clearly Mary Shelley at this point in her life; at the age of nineteen she, like Walton, had lived through failure and was seeking her own future.

In her introduction, Mary recalls that "Many and long were the conversations between Lord Byron and Shelley, to which I was a devout but nearly silent listener." That, of course, is the main function of Walton in the novel — to listen quietly and record Frankenstein's incredible tale. And, in some respects, Frankenstein resembles both Byron and Shelley. Like the persona Byron created for himself, Frankenstein is a haunted, proud, and tortured exile. Walton twice comments on his "full-toned voice [that] swells in my ears . . . a voice whose varied intonations are soul subduing music." Significantly "the impact of Byron's voice upon Mary became . . . almost a symbol for the highly disturbing effect which his personality was able to exert upon her." Walton looks up to Frankenstein as almost a father figure, and Mary Shelley is said to have felt the same way about Byron, selecting him "to play the role of Father, 'unfulfilled since childhood.' " [16] Finally, Frankenstein's marriage to Elizabeth, the "inmate of my parents' house — my more than sister," suggests the event that exiled Byron — his relationship with his half sister, Augusta, with whom he shared a house in Piccadilly. Of course, Frankenstein is not Byron; neither is he Shelley, though there are some biographical parallels we shall examine later. Nevertheless Walton's relationship to Frankenstein is similar to Mary's place in the Byron-Shelley circle. Walton and Mary idealized those they loved, finding for a time that "complete and perfect sympathy" each spent a lifetime seeking. The degeneration and death of Frankenstein reflects Mrs. Shelley's constant fear that her two closest friends or, indeed, anyone she loved, would be lost to her. Her life was something like the Cinderella story; rescued from an "evil" stepmother and stepsisters by a young and handsome prince, Mary Shelley seemed always fearful that the clock was about to strike twelve.

Mrs. Saville and Walton are rather straightforward projections of Mary Shelley, sharing her past and attitudes while staying at the periphery of the action — the place traditionally reserved for Mary. The imaginative center of the novel is, however, with Frankenstein and his Monster. As we shall see, these two figures owe much to Mrs. Shelley's combining of legend and science into a new myth. But they also are the core of her dream and a part of herself. How a reserved young woman could invent such creatures has bothered many who have examined *Frankenstein.* It seems clear that the creation of the Monster is tied to birth and death; this has been seen as growing out of Mary Shelley's pregnancies and miscarriages.[17] It has also been argued that she sees herself as the Monster and William Godwin as the father/creator who abandoned his child.[18] Of course, there is no one answer, but further understanding comes from turning to the dream center of *Frankenstein.*

CHAPTER II

The Waking Dream

The whole series of my life appeared to me as a dream; I some-times doubted if indeed it were all true, for it never presented itself to my mind with the force of reality.

FRANKENSTEIN

ON THE DEEPEST LEVEL, the story Frankenstein tells Walton is a long dream, resonating with the force of nightmare. Mary Shelley began the novel as a dream transcript, starting with the words "It was on a dreary night of November" — what ultimately became chapter five, the creation of the Monster. Since she recalls the dream that inspired it all in an introduction written in 1831, fifteen years after it occurred, better evidence for what actually started her writing is contained in some of the first words she set down. One page into the chapter, Frankenstein himself has a curious dream. Overlooked by nearly everyone who has commented on the novel, this night-mare is the key to understanding the dream world of *Franken-stein* and its relationship to Mary Shelley. Immediately after creating the Monster, Victor Frankenstein lies down to sleep but is "disturbed by the wildest dreams":

> I thought I saw Elizabeth in the bloom of health, walking in the streets of Ingolstadt. Delighted and surprised, I embraced her; but as I imprinted the first kiss on her lips, they became livid with the hue of death; her features appeared to change,

19

and I thought that I held the corpse of my dead mother in my
arms; a shroud enveloped her form, and I saw the graveworms
crawling in the folds of the flannel. I started from my sleep
with horror; a cold dew covered my forehead, my teeth chattered and every limb became convulsed: when, by the dim
and yellow light of the moon as it forced its way through the
window shutters, I beheld the wretch — the miserable monster
whom I had created. He held up the curtain of the bed; and
his eyes, if eyes they may be called, were fixed on me. His
jaws opened, and he muttered some inarticulate sounds, while a
grin wrinkled his cheeks ... I escaped, and rushed downstairs.

In order to interpret this nightmare, we must play psychiatrist and investigate Frankenstein's childhood. Surprisingly,
there is much significant information about his youth in the
novel. In the process of working on *Frankenstein*, Mary
Shelley gave her scientist a revealing past; her awareness of the
importance of this material is made clear in Frankenstein's
preface to his life story:

> ... in drawing the picture of my early days, I also record
> those events which led, by insensible steps, to my after tale of
> misery: for when I would account to myself for the birth of
> that passion, which afterwards ruled my destiny, I find it arise,
> like a mountain river, from ignoble and almost forgotten
> sources; but, swelling as it proceeded, it became the torrent
> which, in its course, has swept away all my hopes and joys.

He remembers his early childhood as idyllic, primarily because he was the center of his parents' universe. His descrip-
tion of these years is full of self-love and a mildly repulsive
emphasis upon the duties owed him by his parents:

> I remained for several years their only child. Much as they
> were attached to each other, they seemed to draw inexhausti-
> ble stores of affection from a very mine of love to bestow

them upon me. My mother's tender caresses, and my father's smile of benevolent pleasure while regarding me, are my first recollections. I was their plaything and their idol, and something better — their child, the innocent and helpless creature bestowed on them by Heaven, whom to bring up to good, and whose future lot it was in their hands to direct to happiness or misery, according as they fulfilled their duties towards me. With this deep consciousness of what they owed towards the being to which they had given life, added to the active spirit of tenderness that animated both, it may be imagined that while during every hour of my infant life I received a lesson of patience, of charity, and of self-control, I was so guided by a silken cord, that all seemed but one train of enjoyment to me.

Frankenstein's idealized infancy is shattered when his mother, desiring a daughter, adopts Elizabeth Lavenza. Frankenstein professes here, as he does throughout the novel, that he loves and adores his new "cousin," his "more than sister." Yet there are hints that he resented sharing his parents' love. He recalls: "Everybody loved Elizabeth. The passionate and almost reverential attachment with which all regarded her became, while I shared it, my pride and my delight." His passionate love for her is combined with a desire to "own" her for life, to declare that "till death she was to be mine only." Elizabeth, the first to enter his household, is the central figure of his nightmare and the last to be murdered by the Monster.

When he is seven years old, a second son, William, is born. Frankenstein places the origin of his desire to probe the mysteries of life and death at this time in his life. Mrs. Shelley clearly ties the inspiration of the young scientist to repressed anger and suggests that his search to explore scientific mysteries is, in part, an exploration of the secrets within himself:

My temper was sometimes violent, and my passions vehement; but by some law in my temperature [disposition] they were turned, not towards childish pursuits, but to an eager desire to learn, and not to learn all things indiscriminately. I confess that neither the structure of languages, nor the code of governments, nor the politics of various states, possessed attractions for me. It was the secrets of heaven and earth that I desired to learn; and whether it was the outward substance of things, or the inner spirit of nature and the mysterious soul of man that occupied me, still my enquiries were directed to the metaphysical, or, in its highest sense, the physical secrets of the world.

At the age of seventeen, as Frankenstein prepares to enter the University of Ingolstadt to continue his studies, an event occurs which he calls "an omen, as it were, of my future misery." His mother dies, and her death is directly caused by Elizabeth. When her foster daughter catches scarlet fever, Frankenstein's mother cannot stay away from her "favorite":

> She attended [Elizabeth's] sickbed — her watchful attentions triumphed over the malignity of the distemper — Elizabeth was saved, but the consequences proved fatal to her preserver. On the third day my mother sickened; her fever was accompanied by the most alarming symptoms, and the looks of the medical attendants prognosticated the worst event. On her death-bed the fortitude and benignity of this best of women did not desert her. She joined the hands of Elizabeth and myself: 'My children,' she said, 'my firmest hopes of future happiness were placed on the prospect of your union ... Elizabeth, my love, you must supply my place to my younger children.'

In one deathbed stroke, Frankenstein's mother sets up a conflict that will only be resolved through the crimes of the Monster. Her former only son must marry Elizabeth to satisfy her dying wish. Though consciously he loves Elizabeth, a part of him hates her for ending his idyllic life as an only child and causing his mother's death. At the same time,

Elizabeth and his mother exchange places — the mother taking Elizabeth's place on the deathbed, while Elizabeth, caring for the children, becomes the mother.

This short case history clarifies Frankenstein's creation dream. The fatal kiss in the dream represents his professed love for Elizabeth and his promise of marriage; her subsequent decomposition suggests his hidden feelings toward her. But she does not merely die. Her transformation into the worm-eaten corpse of his mother shows that he blames Elizabeth for his mother's death and wishes that she had died instead. The dream "argues" that Elizabeth is the one who ought to be rotting in the grave. His desire to exchange life for death, and the hypocrisy of his love, revealed in his dream, help explain his research into life and death and the reason he creates his monster. Frankenstein wakes from this nightmare to see his creation smiling at him in what might be termed a conspiratorial grin, for through the Monster, Frankenstein will achieve all of his dream wishes.

The Monster is, on one level, a dream creature; its creation and crimes resolve the conflict expressed in Frankenstein's nightmare. When Frankenstein first decides to build it, he seems to lose control of his self: "My internal being was in a state of insurrection and turmoil; I felt that order would thence arise, but I had no power to produce it." The Monster itself is a creature of the night, from its birth at one o'clock on a rainy November morning and its nocturnal crimes to its final disappearance, "lost in darkness and distance." We learn that it wears Frankenstein's clothes at the time it tells its maker, "... my form is a filthy type of yours, more horrid even from the very resemblance." This similarity is marred by two additional repulsive qualities — skin that shows the working of arteries and muscles underneath and "dun white" eyes the same color as their sockets. Translucent skin and the apparent lack of pupils are suggestive of a creature that exposes its inner self and looks inward; eyeless creatures often inhabit the dream landscape.

In giving life to this dream double, Frankenstein has purged himself of his anger by projecting it onto another self and thus assured the realization of his secret desires. From the creation on, Frankenstein is without his hatred, full only of guilt, a helpless witness to the decimation of his family. Yet he is always dimly aware that the Monster is himself; he repeatedly confesses to the Monster's crimes, and soon after the creation has what he calls an "obscure feeling" that "There was always scope for fear so long as any thing I loved remained behind." His clearest insight comes soon after the Monster's first murder, when he says, "I considered the being whom I had cast among mankind, and endowed with the will and power to effect purposes of horror ... nearly in the light of my own vampire, my own spirit let loose from the grave, and forced to destroy all that was dear to me." The image of a ghostly spirit, rising from underground like a vampire, fits the nature of his creation. Frankenstein describes his feelings as he discovers the secret of life as like being "buried with the dead" and finding a passage to life. The Monster, resurrected from the remnants of the dead, embodies all those destructive impulses long buried within its creator. It has been argued that Frankenstein's crime is that he abandoned the Monster — for the Monster is not an independent being. When he runs from his creature in horror, Frankenstein fails to take responsibility for himself. But he cannot escape so easily. The rest of the novel chronicles his slowly dawning comprehension that he is living in his own nightmare.

Soon after the creation, while recovering from the first of his many long illnesses, Frankenstein receives a letter from Elizabeth, reminding him of the entry of Justine Moritz, a servant "adopted" into the Frankenstein family. This rather contrived bit of plotting makes sense only when we realize that Frankenstein thus learns two more clues to the nature of the Monster and himself. First, we learn that before her adoption,

> This girl [Justine] had always been the favourite of her father; but through a strange perversity, her mother could not endure her, and, after the death of M. Moritz, treated her very ill. My aunt [Victor's mother] observed this; and when Justine was twelve years of age, prevailed on her mother to allow her to live at our house ... One by one, her [Justine's] brothers and sister died; and her mother, with the exception of her neglected daughter, was left childless ... She sometimes begged Justine to forgive her unkindness, but much oftener accused her of having caused the death of her brothers and sister.

Here Mrs. Shelley introduces, right after Frankenstein's dream, the case of someone accused of willing the death of her family through some hidden hatred. These deaths conveniently leave Justine as an only child — a foreshadowing, perhaps, of the purpose behind the Monster's murders. At the same time, we learn that Justine has also come between Frankenstein and his memory of an exclusive relationship with his mother. One small detail provides the second clue. Like Elizabeth, who symbolically replaces Frankenstein's mother, Justine is described as imitating his mother's "phraseology and manners" so that she often reminds others of her. It is little wonder she will be the Monster's second victim.

The first victim is little William, whose murder is announced in a letter to Frankenstein more than a year after the Monster's creation. In the letter, we learn that William was wearing a miniature of Frankenstein's mother which is now missing; his father speculates that this "was doubtless the temptation which urged the murderer to the deed." Much later, when the Monster itself recounts the murder, it claims that the portrait "in spite of my malignity . . . softened and attracted me. For a few moments I gazed with delight on her dark eyes, fringed by deep lashes, and her lovely lips; but presently my rage returned: I remembered that I was for ever deprived of the delights that such beautiful creatures could bestow, and that she whose resemblance I contemplated would, in regarding me, have changed that air of divine benignity to one expressive of disgust and affright." The Monster takes the locket and, finding Justine sleeping in a barn, makes the puzzling declaration that "the crime had its source in her; be hers the punishment!" It plants the portrait in Justine's dress, thus assuring her execution for William's murder.

This collection of events could be explained as either coincidence or awkward plotting, but, knowing the logic of Frankenstein's nightmare, it takes on a clear meaning. The literal image of Frankenstein's mother is behind two of the Monster's murders. Frankenstein's dream self, in the form of the Monster, believes that if his mother could see the shape of his true "monstrous" feelings, she would reject him. At the same time, he cannot bear to share his idealized memory of his mother's love (symbolized by the locket) with anyone else. So William dies for wearing the locket, and his stepsister Justine is punished ironically through the locket for having "taken" his mother's love. It becomes clearer why Frankenstein is immediately aware of the Monster's guilt but never tells anyone. As he watches Justine's execution, Frankenstein comes closer to self-knowledge, confessing (to himself of course) that "I, the true murderer, felt the never dying worm alive in my bosom which allowed of no hope or consolation." The execution of the innocent Justine is the beginning of the end of Frankenstein's innocence.

The only murder which doesn't seem to fit this pattern is the death of Clerval, who, though the closest companion of Frankenstein's childhood, is not a member of his family. His murder is a puzzle even to Frankenstein, who, in one of his characteristic confessions, blurts out at one point, "Two I have destroyed; other victims await their destiny: but you, Clerval, my friend, my benefactor — " The explanation for his death derives from another aspect of the Monster itself. Frankenstein sought preeminence in his quest for the secrets of life; he hoped to "pioneer a new way, explore unknown powers, and unfold to the world the deepest mysteries of creation." This megalomania is, in part, only the public expression of his deep desire to be first again in his parents' world. The "dream logic" worked out through his Monster is simple — it destroys all the rivals and substitutes for his parents' affection. But it must also destroy Frankenstein's moral side. Henry Clerval becomes, in the novel, a symbol for Frankenstein's moral self; his death makes possible the fulfillment of Frankenstein's nightmare.

From the beginning, Clerval is associated with altruism and preoccupied with chivalry, hardship, and danger: "He composed heroic songs, and began to write many a tale of knightly adventure. He tried to make us act plays, and enter into masquerades, in which the characters were drawn from the heroes of Roncesvalles, of the Round Table, and the chivalrous train who shed their blood to redeem the holy sepulchre from the hands of the infidels." Clerval is, then, a knight — the perfect friend, public benefactor, and adventurer, who "occupied himself, so to speak, with the moral relations of things." Frankenstein once calls him "the image of my former self." [1] One of Clerval's functions in the novel is repeatedly to remind Frankenstein of his need to love man and nature. After Frankenstein creates the Monster, Clerval visits him in Ingolstadt and lectures him on his failure to respond to his family's letters. Later, they travel together through England and Scotland. While Frankenstein is continually looking over his shoulder for the Monster, Clerval busies himself with plans to aid mankind through colonization and trade. The influence of Clerval emerges after Frankenstein goes off by himself to build the Monster's mate. He persuades himself to destroy it with Clerval-like arguments: "Had I a right, for my own benefit, to inflict this curse upon everlasting generations? . . . for the first time the wickedness of my promise burst upon me; I shuddered to think that the future ages might curse me as their pest, whose selfishness had not hesitated to buy its own peace at the price, perhaps, of the existence of the whole human race." The Monster's response is to make Clerval victim number three.

With the death of Clerval, Frankenstein's short-lived moral concern is forgotten. The Monster has forewarned him of his final murder by promising to be with him on his wedding night, yet he feels "a kind of calm forgetfulness, of which the human mind is by its structure peculiarly susceptible." Later he speculates that "as if possessed of magic powers, the monster had blinded me to his real intentions." But no magic is needed to explain this sudden change of feeling. Within the dream logic of the story, the reasons are clear. The death of Clerval is the surrender of Frankenstein's moral self. Despite the Monster's warning, Frankenstein prepares for his marriage with Elizabeth and the final acting out of his dream. Clerval was a knight, living a modern version of chivalry. After his death, Frankenstein acts most unchivalrously, abandoning his lady to the Monster.

When Frankenstein and Elizabeth enter an inn after their wedding boat trip, he leaves his bride to search for the Monster, having convinced himself that it means to kill him. He finds nothing and begins to believe that the Monster has, through some fortunate accident, met its end, when he hears a scream:

> As I heard it, the whole truth rushed into my mind, my arms dropped; the motion of every muscle and fibre was suspended;

28

I could feel the blood trickling in my veins, and tingling in the extremities of my limbs. This state lasted but for an instant; the scream was repeated, and I rushed into the room... what I now held in my arms had ceased to be the Elizabeth whom I had loved and cherished. The murderous mark of the fiend's grasp was on her neck, and the breath had ceased to issue from her lips.

While I still hung over her in an agony of despair, I happened to look up. The windows of the room had before been darkened, and I felt a kind of panic on seeing the yellow light of the moon illuminate the chamber. The shutters had been thrown back; and, with a sensation of horror not to be described, I saw at the open window a figure most hideous and abhorred. A grin was on the face of the monster; he seemed to jeer, as with his fiendish finger he pointed towards the corpse of my wife.

This scene is the culmination of the wishes in Frankenstein's creation nightmare and, in some ways, a replay of it. Some of the details — the corpse of Elizabeth, the yellow light of the moon through the window shutters, and the Monster, grin and all — are identical. Its outstretched hand has been reduced to a "fiendish finger," but the meaning of the gesture is clear. Frankenstein/Monster have acted out their dream; the nightmare has become reality. The "whole truth" Frankenstein realizes is contained in his sudden awareness of his blood running through his veins and tingling in his limbs. The Monster comes from inside himself.

After each of the Monster's murders, Frankenstein suffers from a prolonged period of delirium, punctuated by nightmares in which the Monster tries to destroy him. This final expression of his inner hatred and the horrible realization it brings send him to an insane asylum, where he remembers only darkness, chains, and dreams of wandering in "flowery meadows and pleasant vales with the friends of my youth."

When he is released, Frankenstein is "possessed by a maddening rage." He finally attempts to tell the police of his Monster, but his fantastic story and overwhelming anger convince the magistrate that he is indeed insane. At last, over the graves of the Monster's victims, he swears eternal hatred and revenge. The response is from close by; the Monster's voice whispers in his ear, "I am satisfied; miserable wretch; you have determined to live, and I am satisfied." The final journey across Eastern Europe and Russia to the Arctic plays out the concern with self that drives Frankenstein; before the creation of the Monster this concern blinds him to the implications of his research, and, afterward, it blinds him to the truth behind the Monster's crimes. Now he is similarly self-possessed, this time with self-hatred and self-destruction. Frankenstein has slowly become trapped in his own nightmare, until he is finally caught in a standard dream scene — an endless pursuit over a barren landscape. Day and night are reversed, so that he can recall, "Often, when wearied by a toilsome march, I persuaded myself that I was dreaming until night should come, and that I should then enjoy reality in the arms of my dearest friends ... At such moments, vengeance, that burned within me, died in my heart, and I pursued my path toward the destruction of the daemon more as a task enjoined by heaven, as the mechanical impulse of some power of which I was unconscious, than as the ardent desire of my soul." Despite his ability to wield godlike power, Frankenstein is still a pawn to the greater powers within himself. He ends his nightmare as it had begun, gripped by inner forces that lead him to disaster.

The dream level of *Frankenstein* is not evident at first reading, but it infuses the tale with a nightmare texture that finds its echo in the dreams of us all. The jealousy, hatred, and rivalry that trigger Frankenstein's dream fantasies of murder are common — perhaps universal. The narcissism that leads to the decimation of Frankenstein's family, his "gloomy and narrow reflections upon self," is no more or less than the preeminence we have each felt owed to ourselves. His dream demand for the exclusive right to his mother's love, as well as the desire to replace his siblings for his dead mother, is so common as to be commonplace. The nightmare realm of Frankenstein is, like most nightmares, a world of rage directed at those closest to the dreamer. Monsters, the creatures of nightmare, are objectifications of this rage, or other sexual or aggressive feelings we fear. In a typical dream described by J. A. Hadfield, a monster was first a child's anger urging him to murder and then the projection of his self-hatred threatening to destroy him. The child was jealous of his baby brother and felt he wanted to strangle him. As he recalled his dream, the monster kills his brother, and, then, "I seem to see that *I* was being strangled. I seem to see an ugly form of a man telling me to be a good boy, and if I don't he may destroy *me*. He looks very vicious, a monster. He seems to get *me* by the neck. I scream and wake up and have a terrible sense of guilt for all these thoughts I've been having ... [The Monster] is myself; it is the self I was frightened of urging me to do something I don't want to do." [2]

Frankenstein, then, lives through everyone's nightmares. Mary Shelley's interest in creating a tale that would "speak to the mysterious fears of our nature, and awaken thrilling horror" resulted in a story that draws its power from deep within each of us. She also once wrote, "... above all, let me fearlessly descend into the remotest caverns of my own mind, carry the torch of self-knowledge into its dimmest recesses ..." [3] How conscious she was of the meaning of her dream transcript and its elaboration in the novel is beside the point. Frankenstein's dream world is her world; his terrifying journey of self-discovery also leads deep into the mind of Mary Shelley.

It would be presumptuous to go too far in psychoanalyzing the author through her novel. But the temptation is strong.

Like Victor Frankenstein, Mary Godwin was a first-born child who had to share the household with a collection of adopted siblings and a natural younger brother named William. However, Frankenstein remembers an idyllic childhood. Mary Godwin had no such past — only a well-cultivated worship of her mother's memory and, no doubt, fantasies of a childhood that might have been. In the novel, Elizabeth is given life by Frankenstein's mother but causes her death in the process. She thus becomes the object of Frankenstein's dream hatred and the Monster's final victim. In "real" life, Mary similarly replaced her mother, indirectly causing her death. She was even given her mother's name. Frankenstein's nightmare and the Monster's crimes may well stem from Mary Shelley's deepest conflict. She is both Elizabeth and Frankenstein, acting out her self-hatred and guilt. Her lifelong fear that those she loved would die may have begun with the death of Mary Wollstonecraft, while Harriet Shelley's suicide during the composition of *Frankenstein* may have reinforced a feeling that wishes indeed can kill. As Frankenstein, she creates a Monster that can both vent her hatred toward her family and punish herself. The impossible goal is to expiate her guilt for killing her mother while releasing the rage born of the knowledge that her mother's death made an idyllic childhood only a fantasy. The pattern of the Monster's murders acts to isolate Frankenstein as well as eliminate all those that came between him and his natural parents; the completion of his dream design finishes his task of self-destruction.

The Monster itself can be seen as the most terrifying of Mary Shelley's self-revelations. The embodiment of her deepest anger and loneliness, it is the part of herself she fears others will find hideous and abominable. Abandoned early in life, the Monster is both pathetic and dangerous, doomed always to be outside of the circle of human warmth, peering in from the cold and darkness. We can get some idea of the sources of Mary Shelley's Monster when we realize that William was the name of her two-year-old son, as well as the name of her father and younger brother. Like the character in the novel, Mary's "little Willmouse" was a fair, blue-eyed child. While her "sweet babe" slept in the next room, Mary Shelley wrote of the Monster's murder of his namesake:

> The child still struggled, and loaded me with epithets which carried despair to my heart; I grasped his throat to silence him, and in a moment he lay dead at my feet.
>   I gazed on my victim, and my heart swelled with exultation and hellish triumph.

Of course, such fantasies are not foreign to any parent. But, given the attitudes of the time, Mary Shelley's own neglect as a child, and the death of her daughter, Clara, such thoughts must have seemed to her to be monstrous in the extreme.

However, we must be careful not to attribute too much of the power of the novel to what Muriel Spark called its "implicit utterance." [4] Mary Shelley's moods of brooding and anger, and her feelings of exclusion and self-hatred, were more than sufficient to give birth to both Frankenstein and the Monster. But, once given life, it took the intellect of a remarkable young woman to relate them to larger themes and turn them from self-projections to figures in a modern myth.

CHAPTER III

Double Vision

Invention, it must be humbly admitted, does not consist in creating out of void, but out of chaos; the materials must, in the first place, be afforded: it can give form to dark, shapeless substances, but cannot bring into being the substance itself ... Invention consists in the capacity of seizing on the capabilities of a subject, and in the power of moulding and fashioning ideas suggested to it.

MARY SHELLEY

ALTHOUGH THE IMPETUS for *Frankenstein* was Mary Shelley's dream vision and its implications, she was more than an unconscious writer, automatically transcribing her fantasies. In a grisly and oddly appropriate image, her friend Edward Trelawny once commented on her "fine intellect," saying, "her head might be put upon the shoulders of a Philosopher." [1] Claire Clairmont told her, "You could write upon metaphysics, politics, jurisprudence, astronomy, mathematics — all those highest subjects which [the men] taunt us with being incapable of treating, and surpass them." [2] The men who have commented upon *Frankenstein* in critical journals and books have tended to disparage Mary Shelley's capability for independent thought. She has often had to take the blame for *Frankenstein*'s deficiencies (notably a lack of humor and an excess of sentimentality) and surrender credit for its remarkable strengths to the men who surrounded her. Mario Praz's

34

comment is typical: "All Mrs. Shelley did was to provide a passive reflection for some of the wild fantasies which, as it were, hung in the air around her." [3] Philip Wade, who finds some merit in *Frankenstein*, concludes that it was "more surely a product of Shelley's thought than her own." [4] All this despite Mrs. Shelley's own philosophical independence and her declaration that "I certainly did not owe the suggestion of one incident, nor scarcely of one train of feeling, to my husband, and yet but for his incitement, it would never have taken the form in which it was presented to the world. From this declaration I must except the preface. As far as I can recollect, it was entirely written by him."

Shelley's preface to the 1818 edition implies that he did not agree with the attitudes expressed in his wife's novel. He is careful to state (posing as the author) that "The opinions which naturally spring from the character and situation of the hero are by no means to be conceived as existing always in my own conviction; nor is any inference justly to be drawn from the following pages as prejudicing any philosophical doctrine of whatever kind." He ends her ghostwritten preface with a reference to the ghost story contest and a lame excuse for the fact that she won: "Two other friends (a tale from the pen of one of whom would be far more acceptable to the public than any thing I can ever hope to produce) and myself agreed to write each a story, founded on some supernatural occurrence.

"The weather, however, suddenly became serene; and my two friends left me on a journey among the Alps, and lost, in the magnificent scenes which they present, all memory of their ghostly visions. The following tale is the only one which has been completed." Although it is clear from what remains that Byron, Shelley, and Polidori began conventional tales of terror, Mary Shelley turned to her own nightmares for inspiration. But she was influenced by the Gothic tradition, which also employed dream images to explore the potential of the human mind. In fact, she used the horror tale as a vehicle to connect her private fantasies with her larger fears of the dangers uncovered by the new science. Her essentially Gothic vision of the future contrasts sharply with the optimism of those around her and shows that although she may have sat silently in the presence of Byron and Shelley, her novel speaks clearly with a voice that is all her own.

As she recalls it, the contest began when,

> Some volumes of ghost stories . . . fell into our hands. There was the History of the Inconstant Lover, who, when he thought to clasp the bride to whom he had pledged his vows, found himself in the arms of the pale ghost of her whom he had deserted. There was the tale of the sinful founder of his race, whose miserable doom it was to bestow the kiss of death on all the younger sons of his fated house, just when they reached the age of promise. His gigantic, shadowy form, clothed like the ghost in Hamlet, in complete armour, but with the beaver up, was seen at midnight, by the moon's fitful beams, to advance slowly along the gloomy avenue. The shape was lost beneath the shadow of the castle walls; but soon a gate swung back, a step was heard, the door of the chamber opened, and he advanced to the couch of the blooming youths, cradled in healthy sleep. Eternal sorrow sat upon his face as he bent down and kissed the forehead of the boys, who from that hour withered like flowers snapt upon the stalk. I have not seen these stories since then; but their incidents are as fresh in my mind as if I had read them yesterday.
>
> "We will each write a ghost story," said Lord Byron; and his proposition was acceded to.

The alert reader will notice that the stories, as she remembers them, bear some similarity with the Frankenstein dream; there is a "kiss of death," a bride who becomes a ghost, some

interfamilial murder, and a "gigantic" and presumably monstrous specter. That Mrs. Shelley's memory of the stories is
actually faulty[5] suggests either that her dream influenced her
recollection or (more likely) that such stories were so numerous and interchangeable it would be quite impossible to
remember any individual stories accurately after fifteen years.
Her journal shows she read extensively in the tradition; like
many of her contemporaries, she was addicted to the pseudo-
medievalism and supernaturalism of the tale of terror. She
also read semi-Gothic works such as her father's *Caleb Williams, St. Leon,* and *Fleetwood* and Charles Brockden Brown's
Wieland and *Edgar Huntly,* which replaced ghosts and
castles with a more subtle brand of psychological horror.
Frankenstein reflects this Gothic tradition in the characterization of scientist and Monster, the pattern of pursuit that unites
them both, and the persistent feeling of evil close at hand.

A subspecies of Gothicism played directly upon the theme
of the divided self; derived from ancient and nearly universal
legend, the Doppelgänger tale may well have helped Mrs.
Shelley give form to her dream vision of self-destruction.
Such tales were popular at the time and were certainly among
the "volumes of ghost stories translated from the German"
read around the fire that summer. They all follow the same
formula. The hero (often a monk or student) makes some
sort of infernal pact which releases his double. This other
self is always male and resembles the main character down to
the smallest detail; it usually first appears as the reflection in
a pool or mirror. The double tries to take the place of the
hero, sometimes appearing at his job or committing crimes in
his name but most often trying to steal his lover. Finally, in
order to rid himself of the double, the hero pursues and murders him. Unfortunately, since the double is an inextricable
part of the self, this "self-murder" is suicidal. In a few luckier
instances, the hero wakes up to discover that it was either all

a dream or that he is in an insane asylum. This pattern of creation, rivalry, pursuit, and "self-murder" is as old as folklore; it shows up later in fiction from America (Poe's "William Wilson") to Russia (Dostoevski's *The Double*), and, of course, in the 1890s in England in Stevenson's novella *The Strange Case of Dr. Jekyll and Mr. Hyde*. More to the point, it was a part of the literary tradition that surrounded Mrs. Shelley. Shelley's early Gothic romance, *St. Irvyne* (1810), concludes with the revelation that the two main characters are projections of one self. The double appears in Wordsworth's *The Borderers*, Coleridge's *Christabel*, Blake's *Milton*, and less directly in Shelley's "Alastor" and "Epipsychidion," Byron's *Childe Harold*, and Godwin's *Caleb Williams*, where the main character observes, "[Man] is like those twin-births, that have two heads indeed, and four hands; but, if you attempt to detach them from each other, they are inevitably subjected to miserable and lingering destruction." [6] All of these works are on the extensive reading lists Mary Shelley kept for the years 1814–1816. But her acquaintance with Doppelgängers may have been more than literary; she may have believed that the figure of the double had some basis in reality.

The party gathered at the Villa Diodati was familiar with a phenomenon often associated with doubles. Dr. Polidori had written a pamphlet on sleepwalking the previous year which, his diary shows, he discussed with the Shelleys that summer. Interest in somnambulism was in vogue; one question often raised was whether the sleepwalking individual was displaying a second personality. The idea may owe something to John Locke's supposition in his *Essay Concerning Human Understanding* (1690), that

> if it is possible that the soul can, whilst the body is sleeping, have its thinking, enjoyments, and concerns, its pleasure or

pain, apart, which the man is not conscious of, nor partakes in, it is certain that Socrates asleep, and Socrates awake is not the same person; but his soul when he sleeps and Socrates the man, consisting of body and soul, when he is waking, are two persons.[7]

This idea also appears in Brown's *Edgar Huntly* (1799), which Mary Godwin read in 1814, and numerous other Gothic tales. But the Shelleys had a more immediate reason for discussing somnambulism; they were often awakened by the nocturnal ramblings of Claire Clairmont, who, for example, spent two hours of the night of October 13, 1814, walking about in her sleep and "groaning horribly." Shelley himself, though he kept to his bed, often had "disgusting," "odd" or "disturbing" dreams which, unfortunately, Mary never describes further. Shelley's lifelong fear of insanity was no doubt deepened by his dreams, which may have hinted at the "other self" that lay hidden in his personality. Later in his life, he is said to have met his double walking a terrace. It stopped him and asked, "How long do you mean to be content?"

These subjective experiences of another self seemed at the time to be getting some scientific confirmation. Mrs. Shelley refers to the experiments of Erasmus Darwin in her introduction to *Frankenstein*. Given her interest in science, and the wide familiarity with Darwin's ideas, due largely to his "popularizing" book *Zoonomia, or the Laws of Organic Life* (1794), it is quite possible she may have heard of some of his studies of what he called "double-mindedness." In *Zoonomia*, he writes of a "very elegant and ingenious lady" who "in her days of disease . . . took up the same kind of ideas which we had conversed about on the alternate day before, and could recollect nothing of them on her well days; she appeared to her friends to possess two minds." [8] Elsewhere we read of a

39

young girl who when "not her normal self" reverted to sadistic actions toward her usually beloved sister, and morbid thoughts ("I love the color black, a little wider and longer, and even this [shoe] might make me a coffin").[9]

A more notorious experimenter into the mysteries of the personality was Franz Anton Mesmer (1734–1815). He and his followers conducted research into what is now known as hypnotism in a way that caused a sensation in Europe. In mass "mesmerizing sessions" they stimulated bizarre behavior in otherwise normal subjects; their activities became the center of a quasireligious cult, The Societe de l'Harmonie. Under Mesmer's trance, "unfamiliar impulses appeared, foreign to the patient's usual character, as if revealing a second personality, which might even be the reverse of the first."[10] Mesmer jealously guarded the secret of his power, which made him the object of fear and awe, "closer to the ancient magician than the twentieth century psychiatrist."[11] His techniques were studied, derided, imitated, and exaggerated; he was believed able to cure a variety of diseases and after his death, "saint's stories" were told of his power to mesmerize birds and animals. It is quite likely that Mrs. Shelley, living in Switzerland the year after his death, not far from his home in Meersburg, heard much of his achievements and legend. His uncanny power to draw what seemed to be another self out of sleeping subjects may have not only convinced her of the reality of the double self but also may have hinted of the use the new science might make of such knowledge.

As should be obvious by now, the tradition of the double is echoed in *Frankenstein*, although the novel is not strictly a double tale. Some of the more obvious connections are the general pattern of creation, pursuit, and self-destruction, the visionary nature of the Monster's nocturnal appearances, and Frankenstein's periodic bouts of unconsciousness, which coincide with the Monster's attacks. There is, as well, the competition for love common to double tales; when Frankenstein destroys the Monster's bride, his own bride is doomed. But the tradition is particularly interesting as a connection between Mrs. Shelley's private nightmare and her conservatism about the future promised by science. This can be seen by tracing a set of images that begins in her dream and threads through the novel.

Mary Shelley ends her account of her waking dream by referring to some details so vivid that, in her words, "I see them still; the very room, the dark *parquet*, the closed shutters, with moonlight struggling through, and the sense I had that the glassy lake and white high Alps were beyond." We have already seen the closed shutters and moonlight in Frankenstein's creation dream, while the Alpine glaciers become the refuge of the Monster. But one other detail is of interest — the "glassy lake." Although Mary Shelley was subject to severe seasickness throughout her life and looked upon ocean journeys with dread, all of *Frankenstein* is set aboard Walton's ship, and within that frame the motif of boats drifting on water constantly returns. The powerful personal horror that the image must have held for the author is not for most of us to share, but the use she made of it has a wider meaning. Serving much the same function as the mirror in double tales, the symbol of water suggests the depths of Mrs. Shelley's "placid" personality, the gradual surrender of Frankenstein to his dream double, and, in a larger sense, the loss of control of science to the technological "doubles" it creates.

Water is, from the beginning, linked to Frankenstein's mental state. Returning to Geneva after creating the Monster, he looks at the lake and wonders at the significance of its appearance: "The sky and lake are blue and placid. Is this to prognosticate peace, or mock at my unhappiness?" He arrives home too late to enter town (the gates are locked) so he must cross the lake in a boat to get to Plainpalais. The turn of plot seems unnecessary, yet it serves to introduce the image, as well as Frankenstein's first postcreation view of the Monster. Aboard the boat, he watches a lightning storm "illuminating the lake, making it appear like a vast sheet of fire." He disembarks near his home and, in a flash of lightning, sees the Monster for the first time since he abandoned it. Soon after, Justine is executed for William's murder and, wracked with guilt, Frankenstein heads back to the lake:

> Often, after the rest of the family had retired for the night, I took the boat, and passed many hours upon the water. Sometimes, with my sails set, I was carried by the wind; and sometimes, after rowing into the middle of the lake, I left the boat to pursue its own course, and gave way to my own miserable reflections. I was often tempted, when all was at peace around me, and I the only unquiet thing that wandered restless in a scene so beautiful and heavenly — if I except some bat, or the frogs, whose harsh and interrupted croaking was heard only when I approached the shore — often, I say, I was tempted to plunge into the silent lake, that the waters might close over me and my calamities for ever.

These suicidal impulses recur when, soon after this, he meets and talks with the Monster and returns to pass "whole days on the lake alone in a little boat, watching the clouds, and listening to the rippling of the waves, silent and listless."

The image of a boat "pursuing its own course" on water, a common Romantic motif,[12] suggests man allowing his unconscious self to control him — letting the boat drift where it will. Water is, of course, an ancient symbol of the depths of the mind. The act of letting the boat wander far from the disturbing sounds of the conscious world of man and nature on the shore is in one sense an abandoning of outward concern — literally giving way to "my own miserable reflections."

Double Vision

Otto Rank sees narcissism at the heart of the concept of the double; the preoccupation with self in double tales is actually a "pathological fear of one's self, often leading to paranoid insanity and appearing personified in the pursuing shadow, mirror-image, or double." [13] The temptation of Frankenstein to "plunge into the silent lake" is paralleled in Doppelgänger tales; there the hero is often drawn, not to the water, but to a mirror, and threatened with absorption by his mirror image. Often, he loses his reflection when his other self takes form and is consequently afraid to look in a mirror. In E. T. A. Hoffmann's tale "The Sandman," for example, the hero believes "there is a dark power, hostile and treacherous, which lays within our inmost being a thread, by which it can then catch hold of us, and draw us forth on a dangerous and fatal path which we should otherwise not have taken — if there is such a power, it must, within us, take our own form, and indeed become our very self . . . If we have sufficient firmness of character . . . then this uncanny power perishes as it vainly strives to assume the form of our own mirror-reflection." [14] As he loses control over his other self, Victor Frankenstein comes inexorably closer to being drawn into the mirror world of the sea.

Despondent over the deaths of Justine and William, he travels to Chamounix, a village in the French Alps. After a restful night, lulled to sleep by the rushing of the Arve River, Frankenstein climbs a glacier, the Mer de Glace, and finally arrives at a "vast river of ice" with a surface "like the waves of a troubled sea" glittering in the sunlight. Alone in this mirror landscape, he calls upon the supernatural: "Wandering spirits . . . allow me this faint happiness, or take me, as your companion, away from the joys of life." As if in answer to his invocation, at that moment he meets the Monster again, a gigantic form striding easily over the crevices in the ice. After the Monster's lengthy story, Frankenstein returns to Geneva

43

and soon sets out with Clerval on a journey up the Rhine. Frankenstein "lay at the bottom of the boat" recalling, "as I gazed on the cloudless blue sky, I seemed to drink in a tranquillity to which I had long been a stranger."

When he arrives at the Orkney Islands to build the second Monster, he again is surrounded by water. He describes the place he selects for his laboratory as "a place fitted for such a work, being hardly more than a rock, whose high sides were continually beaten upon by the waves." Since there are only five people on the island, it really isn't a fit place to create another monster — the cemeteries, charnel houses, and other "body shops" are missing. But symbolically it is a fit place, for by now the Monster is gaining in power; the location of the new laboratory hints at Frankenstein's loss of control as he submits to a stronger, more elemental, and rebellious dream self. He compares the waves of this ocean to the lake he has left: "[Switzerland's] fair lakes reflect a blue and gentle sky; and when troubled by winds, their tumult is but as the play of a lively infant, when compared to the roarings of the giant ocean."

The Monster has not been seen during Frankenstein's slow journey through Germany and England, though he has always been aware of it somewhere on the edge of his perception. Its return, after he destroys the nearly completed Monster bride, is heralded by another dreamlike use of water. This scene again suggests the surrender of the conscious mind to a creature from the depths, using the same pattern as before:

> Several hours passed, and I remained near my window gazing on the sea; it was almost motionless, for the winds were hushed, and all nature reposed under the eye of the quiet moon. A few fishing vessels alone specked the water, and now and then the gentle breeze wafted the sound of voices, as the fishermen called to one another. I felt the silence, although I was hardly conscious of its extreme profundity, un-

til my ear was suddenly arrested by the paddling of oars near
the shore and a person [the Monster] landed close to my
house.

The same curious elements recur: half-heard sounds of "reality," an overwhelming silence, the slipping away of awareness, and the mirrorlike water. The repetition of the image
in all of its detail before the Monster's second murder suggests
that it may function as a kind of trigger, heralding a loss of
control over the double as it emerges from the depths of his
unconscious to strike at those around him.

This impression is intensified immediately after this when
the enraged Monster gets back into its own boat, which "shot
across the waters with an arrowy swiftness, and was soon
lost amidst the waves." Frankenstein decides (again) to commit suicide, then to pass his life on the barren island, kept
from the rest of humanity by the sea "which I almost regarded as an insuperable barrier between me and my fellow-
creatures." Instead, that night he puts to sea in a small skiff
and again surrenders to the waves: "I resolved to prolong my
stay on the water; and, fixing the rudder in a direct position,
stretched myself at the bottom of the boat. Clouds hid the
moon, everything was obscure, and I heard only the sound
of the boat, as its keel cut through the waves; the murmur
lulled me, and in a short time I slept soundly." When he last
allowed the wind to carry his boat, he was safe; on the ocean
it is different. He awakens to discover that the waves "continually threatened the safety of my little skiff. I found that
the wind was north-east, and must have driven me far from
the coast from which I had embarked. I endeavoured to
change my course, but quickly found out that, if I again
made the attempt, the boat would be instantly filled with
water. Thus situated, my only resource was to drive before
the wind. I confess that I felt a few sensations of terror."

45

He lands on an Irish beach and is immediately arrested for the murder of Henry Clerval. The chief witness to the crime is Daniel Nugent, who "swore positively that . . . he saw a boat, with a single man in it, at a short distance from shore; and, as far as he could judge by the light of a few stars, it was the same boat in which I [Frankenstein] had just landed."

The image of boats and water not only ties the two sides of scientist-monster together — it also chronicles the transfer of power from maker to Monster. Thus, when Frankenstein and his father leave Ireland, the young scientist who had such bright dreams of power has shrunk to a virtual ghost: "I was a shattered wreck — the shadow of a human being. My strength was gone. I was a mere skeleton . . . We took our passage on board a vessel bound for Havre-de-Grace, and sailed with a fair wind . . . It was midnight. I lay on the deck looking at the stars and listening to the dashing of the waves. . . . The past appeared to me in the light of a frightful dream, yet the vessel in which I was, the wind that blew me from the detested shore of Ireland, and the sea which surrounded me, told me too forcibly that I was deceived by no vision." Vessel, wind, and sea are but further reminders of the hidden self that has robbed him of his life and strength, and waits to emerge once more and lead him to his final voyage.

In each instance, water has lulled Frankenstein's defenses and announced the appearance of the Monster. On his wedding day, Frankenstein and Elizabeth journey by boat to an inn on a lake. He tells his bride, who is melancholy with a "presentiment of evil," to "Look also at the innumerable fish that are swimming in the clear waters, where we can distinguish every pebble that lies at the bottom. What a divine day!" The water no longer reflects his self; its clarity seems to suggest that Frankenstein's unconscious hides nothing. This self-delusion allows the Monster to strangle his bride. Frankenstein, who has lost consciousness for precisely the minute of the murder, rushes into his room in time to see his creature run "with the swiftness of lightning" and plunge, of course, into the lake. He faints again and awakens "hardly conscious of what happened; my eyes wandered around the room, as if to seek something that I had lost." He returns to Geneva, by boat, but the wind is unfavorable, and he is forced to row all night. While on the lake, he realizes his hope of happiness and forgetfulness was itself a foolish dream and begins the world-spanning pursuit of his creature that ends in the death of both. By the end of this journey, the boat has become a sledge, and the water, a limitless "frozen Ocean." Frankenstein himself is drowned in rage and hatred, which "like a mighty tide, overwhelmed every other feeling." On a vast mirror landscape of ice, he pursues his elusive Monster, seeking the self-murder that will lead to his own release. The Monster, meanwhile, leaves food and instructions for its pursuer, leading him further and further into coldness and isolation. It realizes that their lives are inextricably linked. One of its notes reads: "My reign is not yet over . . . you live, and my power is complete." The narcissism which led Frankenstein to give life to his Monster and fueled its hatred and his own reaches its climax at the end of his wanderings, as his monomania focuses on the murder of his other self. When Walton spots him, he is on a shrinking piece of ice, about to be engulfed in a "tumultuous sea." The image aptly ends the motif of boats and water, suggesting as it does the fragment of his former self that is rapidly melting away, itself a bit of the frozen ocean. Aboard Walton's own ship, he wishes only for death, the final stop on a voyage that led from self-glorification to self-destruction.

The Doppelgänger theme in *Frankenstein*, epitomized in the image of the self reflected in, and drawn to water and ice, is more than the reworking of a literary tradition or the expression of Mary Shelley's personal conflicts; it is an integral

47

part of the mythic statement of the novel, an insight that helps keep *Frankenstein* alive. Modern theorists such as Otto Rank, C. G. Jung, and R. D. Laing have used something like the concept of the double as a model for the human psyche. Jungian theory points out that "the shadow cast by the conscious mind of the individual contains the hidden, repressed, and unfavorable (or nefarious) aspects of the personality. But this darkness is not just the simple converse of the conscious ego. Just as the ego contains unfavorable or destructive qualities, so the shadow has good qualities — normal instincts and creative impulses. Ego and shadow indeed, although separate, are inextricably linked together." [15] The shadow has also been described as emotional, autonomous, and able to "possess" the ego.[16]

Further understanding comes from observing the actions of the mentally "unbalanced." The onset of schizophrenia has been depicted as heralded by the conscious "enfirming" of the shadow self by the ego, while schizophrenic behavior at times follows Frankenstein's pattern of isolation, degeneration, and self-murder.[17] In fact, Frankenstein could almost be labeled a narcissistic schizophrenic, or what Freud called a paraphrenic: "They suffer from megalomania and have withdrawn their interest from the external world (people and things)." The paraphrenic is also preoccupied with "the lost narcissism of his childhood — the time when he was his own ideal." Such a person constantly watches himself, leading to "so-called delusions of observation, or, more correctly, of *being watched*." [18] The parallels, though provocative, are not an attempt to file maker and Monster into a neat Freudian system but suggest the psychological validity behind the character of Mrs. Shelley's prototypical mad scientist.

The Monster hangs suspended in the tension between the self and the world, the imaginary and the concrete, illusion and reality. Its half-real existence as Frankenstein's dream double has, like the personality of Frankenstein himself, a relationship to actual psychological phenomena. Frankenstein's (and P. B. Shelley's) curious "double vision," although uncommon, is not unknown. Stanley Colman and N. Lukianowicz have examined cases of what Lukianowicz calls "autoscopy" and Colman calls "Capgras' syndrome", or the delusion of seeing one's double.[19] Most of these people see their doubles' faces, or faces and upper torsos, usually no more than a yard or so away. The double often appears at dusk and brings with it sensations of weariness and coldness. With a few exceptions, it has no color, and comes and goes in a few seconds. (I talked to an anthropologist who, while in New Guinea, had just such an experience. He awoke late at night to see the head and torso of a man approaching his bed. With the sudden realization that he was seeing his double, his uneasiness vanished. Thinking "It's only myself" he went back to sleep!) For the unfortunate few, autoscopy is neither a brief nor a pleasant experience. Some people are always aware of their doubles at the edge of their perception, visible by day whenever they close their eyes and by night with their eyes open or shut. Cases exist of multiple doubles, where people have literally seen hundreds of identical copies of themselves. Women, oddly enough, tend to see doubles of men, while men see doubles of themselves — a phenomenon which may explain why feminine doubles are so rare in literature and why both Frankenstein and his Monster are male.

Some recent physiological studies of the human brain have provided the most startling evidence of the two-sided nature of the personality. It has long been known that the two halves of the brain each control the opposite side of the body and that one half (usually the left) dominates. The two sides communicate and coordinate their activities through a network of fibers called the corpus callosum. When these fibers are surgically severed (as is done for very severe cases of

49

epilepsy) the two sides of the brain are put out of communication, sometimes causing bizarre complications. The two halves can take on independent personalities; the right side, which lacks the power of speech, often shows a more "primitive" and nasty character, while the left side, which controls speech and writing, generally displays a more rational and creative disposition. The two "selves" can come into conflict, with quite dangerous results. There is a case on record of a patient who was caught in this struggle: "Once he grabbed his wife with his left hand and shook her violently, while with the right trying to come to his wife's aid in bringing the left belligerent hand under control."

One researcher has concluded that "just as conjoined twins are two different people sharing a common body, the callosum-sectioned human has two separate conscious spheres sharing a common brain stem, head and body." [20] Whether all this means that the two sides of our brains are, in effect, "doubles" kept in uneasy balance through the corpus callosum is open to conjecture. What it does suggest is that the twilight world of Frankenstein/Monster may have its counterpart in the conflicts inherent in the human personality.

The theme of boats and water, like the Doppelgänger motif itself, is an important link between the psychological level of the novel and its scientific prophecy. The end of Frankenstein and his dreams of pouring "a torrent of light into our dark world" resulted from his ignorance of the darkness within himself. The tradition of the double and the power of the mirror self, tied to the revelations of dream and the latest discoveries in the embryonic science of the mind, gave Mary Shelley good reason to fear the direction taken by technology — the new "science of mechanics." In her notes to Shelley's *Prometheus Unbound*, she comments that her husband "believed mankind had only to will that there would be no evil, and there would be none," adding, "it is not my part in these Notes to notice the arguments that have been urged against this opinion, but to mention that he . . . was attached to it with fervent enthusiasm." [21] Her pessimism about the future of man came from a deep awareness that there were greater forces than the will latent in the human personality. Growing out of Mary Shelley's personal fears and fantasies, the Gothic interplay of maker and Monster became the basis for her mistrust of the promises the new science was making.

CHAPTER IV

From Mind to Machine

Mary Shelley wrote in the infancy of modern science, when its enormous possibilities were just beginning to be foreseen by imaginative writers like Byron and Shelley and by speculative scientists like Davy and Erasmus Darwin. At the age of nineteen, she achieved the quietly astonishing feat of looking beyond them...

M. K. JOSEPH

WHEN MARY SHELLEY gave her intended "ghost story" a scientific context, she linked the Gothic concept of the double with technology. Listening to the many long conversations between Byron and Shelley about "the nature of the principle of life, and whether there was any probability of its ever being discovered or communicated," she heard of using electricity to animate a corpse or a "manufactured creature." We might tend to dismiss this speculation, which became the immediate impetus for her vision, as a further manifestation of the Gothic imagination of Shelley and company, especially since it appears to be based upon a supposed experiment of Erasmus Darwin, who was said to have watched a piece of vermicelli in a glass case come to life! But, at the time, the idea of creating life seemed a quite reasonable possibility for the near future. Contemporary scientific theory and some spectacular experiments fueled Byron and Shelley's excitement and, no doubt, Mary Shelley's fear that advances in what was called the "science of mechanics" might actually give man the ability to "manufacture" creatures in his own image — doubles given reality by the power of technology.

Along with the Industrial Revolution arose the belief that mechanical principles governed all phenomena, from the movement of the planets to the beating of a heart. By the nineteenth century, the major scientific thinkers, following Descartes, were proclaiming that all of Nature was one vast machine. As a result, the distinction between the living and the dead was blurred. It was, for example, widely felt that "inorganic matter could easily generate living beings as it was already alive." [1] The search for the power that could give life seemed to have ended with the discovery of galvanism (electricity). One prominent scientist declared that "galvanic phenomena seemed to bridge the gap between living and non-living matter." [2] Such thinking led to the conclusion that the animation of a corpse was merely an electrical problem that more than one researcher set out to solve. In 1803, Giovanni Aldini used electric shock to induce muscle spasms in the corpse of a criminal hanged at Newgate; as in Galvani's famous earlier experiments with the legs of frogs, the momentary twitching induced by the current was mistaken for a short-lived "spark of life." It seemed only a matter of time before a frog (or corpse) would rise resurrected from the galvanist's table.

If men were really machines, then machines could be made into men. Mary Shelley might well have encountered E. T. A. Hoffmann's two short stories "Automatons" (1812) and "The Sandman" (1814) among the German tales she heard; they both deal with clockwork dolls that effectively simulate life. The technique was more than theoretical. Pierre and Henri Jaquet-Droz created three "mechanical puppets" and, in 1774, demonstrated them on a widely publicized tour of the salons and courts of Europe. The small figure known as the Draughtsman could make four different drawings, while the Scribe was able, by the arrangement of a set of cams, to write any text up to forty letters long. Other contemporary automata included Baron Wolfgang Kempelen's chess player, which defeated the Empress of Austria in 1769 (probably a fake), and Jacques de Vaucanson's mechanical duck, which both ate and defecated! The trivial nature of these "robots" makes no less significant the attitude they represented — that the actions of the living could be effectively aped by machines. One consequence of this equation of man and mechanism was an erasure of the moral boundaries between what science could create and what was reserved for a higher technology. In 1789, Johann Friedrich Blumenbach described a method for growing monstrous human embryos resembling frogs, while in 1812 Johann Friedrich Meckel supposed that "the growth of a human embryo might be impeded while it was developing up the scale of organic beings, so that a monstrous child was born." [3] Mary Shelley may not have heard of these particular gruesome speculations, but she was aware of the implications of the new scientific attitude. As Lewis Mumford put it in 1970, "In a world of machines, or of creatures that can be reduced to machines, technocrats would indeed be gods." [4]

Shelley's fascination with the power of science to give life was no doubt linked to his belief in the omnipotence of man and the superfluousness of God. Mrs. Shelley, on the other hand, had quite a different reaction. The terror in her dream comes from the "supremely frightful . . . effect of any human endeavour to mock the stupendous mechanism of the Creator of the world." Her fear of the consequences of attempting to copy the "mechanism" of Nature set her apart from her contemporaries, yet Frankenstein's belated awareness of the disaster that ensues when man "aspires to become greater than his nature will allow" has become a part of the popular myth of technology in the twentieth century. She bases her fears on her awareness of the conflicts in her own nature and her understanding that technology can never be any more than a magnified image of the self. The dangers accompanying such an attempt at transcendence were made clear to Mrs. Shelley when she looked at an ancient tradition that still survived. Just as the new science of the mind gave reality to the legendary concept of the Doppelgänger, the new technology had its old counterpart. The "science" of alchemy also reduced the complexities of Nature to a few simple principles and held out hope that man could use these secrets to gain cosmic power.

In her father's novel *St. Leon* (1799), she read of an alchemist, Reginald St. Leon, who discovers both the philosophers' stone and the elixir of life, believing they will benefit himself and mankind. Instead they bring him isolation, misery, and destruction. The search for these secrets is as old as the fear of death and the love of power; the "science" of alchemy itself has been traced to China and Egypt before the time of Christ. The philosophers' stone (often described not as a stone but as a reddish powder) could supposedly transmute "base" metals to gold. The elixir (often considered a property of the philosophers' stone) gave eternal life. Although alchemists did much to advance man's knowledge of medicine and chemistry, they are most remembered for their fantastic visions of perfection and their part in the ancient struggle for control over nature and death. The medieval alchemist believed that one day, in a primitive laboratory, after repeated purifying, distilling, and refining, he would find the secrets of life and be like God.

Two of the most famous alchemists, Albertus Magnus and Paracelsus, are referred to in *Frankenstein*. They were well known to Shelley, who pored over their works as a boy; considering the nature of the Shelleys' relationship, they were doubtless familiar to Mary as well. Both alchemists were rumored actually to have found the secret of life. Albertus Magnus (1206?–1280), teacher of Thomas Aquinas, supposedly discovered the elixir and used it to animate a brass statue, which learned to speak and became a servant but took on too many human qualities. Rather than working silently, it chattered unendingly. One day, unable to stand its distractions any longer, Thomas Aquinas took up a hammer, smashed it to pieces, and went back to his studies. This early folk tale of man against robot can be contrasted with the famous recipe that Paracelsus (1493–1541) gave for growing a homunculus, or little man, which included human semen, horse manure, and a forty-day incubation period in a sealed glass jar. That the experiments with manufactured creatures and living vermicelli discussed by Byron and Shelley echo these tales is probably no coincidence. Modern science fascinated Shelley and horrified Mary for the same reason — it seemed to bring the old dreams within grasp.

Although the historical Paracelsus and Albertus Magnus lived relatively calm lives, the alchemists and sorcerers of legend and literature often paid dearly for their forbidden knowledge. While there is no evidence that Mary Shelley read Goethe's Faust (Part One was first published in its complete form in 1808, Part Two not until 1832), she was familiar with the figure of the overreacher, who momentarily commands divine power, only to be destroyed because of it. In fact, the subtitle of Frankenstein is The Modern Prometheus and Prometheus is a mythic ancestor of the overreacher. A Titan who, according to legend, made man out of clay and gave him fire stolen from the Gods, Prometheus was a familiar character in Romantic literature. He was punished for his presumption by Zeus, who chained him to a rock in the Caucasus where his liver was eaten daily by a vulture (or eagle in some versions) and renewed every night. In 1819,

Shelley finished *Prometheus Unbound*, a closet drama that freed Prometheus from his rock and made him an heroic rebel he called "the type of the highest perfection of moral and intellectual nature, impelled by the purest and truest motives to the best and noblest ends." [5] There are no direct references to Prometheus in *Frankenstein*, but if Mary Shelley's hero is a "modern Prometheus," then he is a Faustian and not a Shelleyan Prometheus. The subtitle is a reminder of the disastrous consequences of attempting to control higher powers for earthly purposes. Her Promethean scientist plays God, building a creature that he hopes will be the first of a "new species [that] would bless me as its creator and source" but which turns out to be the vulture that carries out his eternal torment.

More obvious Faustian overtones are contained in the occult dabblings of medieval magicians. Cornelius Agrippa, an "ancient author" mentioned in *Frankenstein*, was known as a magician who tried to call up ghosts and demons to do his bidding. The practice is often linked to alchemy, since both involve the search for cosmic power through secret knowledge. Paracelsus, for example, was believed to have kept a demon named Azoth imprisoned in a jewel. Even the Gothic villain was as likely to be a magician as an alchemist. In Matthew Lewis' *The Monk* (1795), Ambrosio, a monk known to the world as "The Man of Holiness," is aided in his decidedly unholy pursuit of Antonia by a magic mirror and the devil himself. Spells and potions were part of the Gothic brew served up in William Beckford's *Vathek* (1786), Veit Weber's *The Sorcerer* (1795), and other delicacies on Mrs. Shelley's reading lists. Invariably, they follow the Faustain pattern; momentary control of superhuman forces is followed by a gruesomely described and inevitably eternal punishment.

It is even possible that Mrs. Shelley got the name "Frankenstein" itself from the legend of an alchemist who gave life to a monster. Two years before she began her novel, Shelley, Mary, and Claire traveled up the Rhine by boat (a journey taken in *Frankenstein*). Along their route, a few miles outside of Darmstadt, Germany, stands Castle Frankenstein. A gaunt, thirteenth-century Gothic ruin perched on a gloomy ridge, it seems the perfect place to spawn legends. In fact, many curious tales are still told about the castle and its inhabitants. A famous German alchemist, Johann Konrad Dippel, was born in the castle in 1673; historically he is known only for the invention of an oil and textile dye. But darker alchemical activities are said to have occupied the Frankenstein family. A Frankenstein was supposed to have returned from the Crusades with a wife who was a sorceress; together they dabbled in things "man is not meant to know." A knight buried on the grounds is said to have died in battle with a ferocious, man-eating monster in the shape of a boar that, according to some versions of the legend, was man-made. Although Mary Shelley's own journal makes no mention of Castle Frankenstein, Claire recalls that, on the first and second of September 1814, the three travelers stopped at some of the numerous ruined castles, "the names of which I do not recollect." [6] Mrs. Shelley evidently remembered the name Frankenstein and used it for her scientist. She also may have heard some of these tales, mixing alchemy with a man-made monster and surrounded by that same Faustian aura of diabolical experimentation and its disastrous outcome.

But alchemy and the occult were more than musty legends. Mrs. Shelley was no doubt familiar with the story of Dr. James Price who, in 1782, published an account of his method of transmuting mercury into gold or silver. His cleverness at fooling learned witnesses (aided, of course, by their willingness to believe) resulted in a short-lived flurry of excitement, culminating in his being honored by Oxford University with a degree and election as a Fellow of the Royal Society. His momentary triumph had its own gruesome punishment. Commanded to perform his transmutation before members of the Society under strictly controlled conditions, he poisoned himself in their presence, dying on July 31, 1783, at the age of twenty-five. At the same time, Comte de Sainte-Germain was in the middle of a long life, reportedly prolonged by the possession of the elusive elixir. Talked about all over Europe, Saint-Germain fed his fantastic reputation — hinting, for example, that he had been present at the Passion of Christ!

Shelley himself was attracted by the ancient dreams. While a student at Eton, he startled his tutors when he tried, literally, to raise Hell. In a letter to Godwin, he remembered how he read "ancient books of Chemistry and Magic . . . with an enthusiasm of wonder, almost amounting to belief." [7] These playful excursions into medievalism were augmented by Shelley's experiments in modern chemistry and physics, for he also possessed a galvanic battery and considerable chemical apparatus. Mary Shelley modeled young Victor Frankenstein on young Percy Shelley; both began with a fascination for alchemy and then learned to use the new science to try to fulfill the old dreams. Her doubts about the outcome of such a search were shaped by her awareness of the meaning of the inevitable conclusion of the Faustian stories and her realization that the very nature of man would insure the transmutation of dream into nightmare.

The education of Victor Frankenstein not only parallels Shelley's changing interests, it follows the history of science from alchemy to modern technology. Frankenstein spends his youth in the medieval world of his first "teachers" — the books of Albertus Magnus, Paracelsus, and Cornelius Agrippa. His purpose was to enter

. . . with the greatest diligence into the search of the philosopher's stone and the elixir of life; but the latter soon obtained my undivided attention. Wealth was an inferior object; but what glory would attend the discovery, if I could banish disease from the human frame, and render man invulnerable to any but a violent death!

Nor were these my only visions. The raising of ghosts or devils was a promise liberally accorded by my favorite authors, the fulfillment of which I most eagerly sought...

His grandiose if somewhat shopworn dreams are rudely exploded by a lightning bolt that destroys a tree near their house in Belrive when he is fifteen years old:

As I stood at the door, on a sudden I beheld a stream of fire issue from an old and beautiful oak, which stood about twenty yards from the house; and so soon as the dazzling light vanished, the oak had disappeared, and nothing remained but a blasted stump. When we visited it the next morning, we found the tree shattered in a singular manner. It was not splintered by the shock, but entirely reduced to thin ribands of wood. I never beheld any thing so utterly destroyed.

A "man of great research in natural philosophy" who is conveniently visiting the family at the time uses the occasion for an impromptu lecture on the new theories of electricity and galvanism. The immediate result is that Frankenstein gives up his medieval studies, believing that nature has far greater power than man can ever hope to control. The real lesson of the shattered tree comes too late. After he uses a technological imitation of God's power, the galvanic "spark of life," to create his Monster, he finds that it, too, can destroy. Much later, he sees deeper: "But I am a blasted tree; the bolt has entered my soul." Only in retrospect does he take the incident as the last heavenly warning of what is to come, the last chance to turn back from a path that led to his own "utter and terrible destruction."

Thus, when he enters Ingolstadt University, Frankenstein

is caught between the old and new science. He has given up the ancient methods but not the ancient dreams; he sees electricity as the secret of cosmic power but feels man can never control it. Then he meets two scientists who show him the two directions his life, and modern science, can take. Professor Krempe ridicules alchemy. He seeks knowledge, not power, and urges Frankenstein to begin anew, to be content with what Frankenstein calls "realities of little worth." But, as he is ready to give up altogether, he wanders into the lecture hall of Professor Waldman. There he learns that modern science can give him the power of the lightning bolt and the promise of succeeding where alchemy and the occult failed.

Waldman bombastically declares,

"The ancient teachers of science ... promised impossibilities and performed nothing. The modern masters promise very little; they know that metals cannot be transmuted, and that the elixir of life is a chimera. But these philosophers, whose hands seem only made to dabble in dirt, and their eyes to pore over the microscope or crucible, have indeed performed miracles. They penetrate into the recesses of nature, and show how she works in her hiding places. They ascend into the heavens; they have discovered how the blood circulates, and the nature of the air we breathe. They have acquired new and almost unlimited powers; they can command the thunders of heaven, mimic the earthquake, and even mock the invisible world with its own shadows."

Even though he begins by attacking the pretensions of the medieval alchemists, it soon becomes clear that Waldman is promising, if not the same secrets, the same power. Krempe saw science as the path to knowledge; Waldman's "new alchemy" uses the achievements of science for technological purposes which seem, unfortunately, to center around literally world-shaking imitations of celestial, natural, and even supernatural power.

His lecture has its effect. Fired with his old zeal, Frankenstein sets out to use modern science to fulfill the dusty dreams of his boyhood. He finds the "elixir of life," described as a sudden knowledge, a "brilliant and wondrous light" that arose from his graveyard research into the nature of life and death. He recognizes his revelation for what it really is, exclaiming in, "what had been the study and desire of the wisest men since the creation of the world was now within my grasp" while at the same time seeing it as magic wrought by modern science — "some miracle might have produced it, though the stages of its discovery were distinct and probable."

A true pupil of Waldman's, his first thought upon acquiring this knowledge is to find some way to use it. He soon, however, must make technological compromises with his godlike decision to create a new species. Because the "minuteness of the parts formed a great hindrance," what began as a man ends as a mockery — a hideous "being of gigantic stature." Built in the bare attic room of his boarding house (the "monstrous engine" of Mrs. Shelley's dream has been discarded), the creature is animated in a fit setting for the occult: "the rain pattered dismally against the panes, and my candle was nearly burnt out when, by the glimmer of the half-extinguished light, I saw the dull yellow eye of the creature open." From then on, he calls it either "daemon" or "devil." Linked to his creation dream, it becomes the ghostly other self destined to decimate his family. Frankenstein uses his modern elixir to raise a creature that is, metaphorically at least, both devil and ghost; at the end of what has been called "a long chain of rational controlled experiments, in the logical manner in which modern science and thought are supposed to proceed" [8] stands a medieval horror.

The impulses behind the "new alchemy" are the same, then,

as those behind the old. The difference is that, for the first time, the new methods seemed to be leading to success. In describing the events leading to the creation of the Monster, Mrs. Shelley shows again her preoccupation with the reflection of the motives of the creator in the things he creates. On this level, the Monster is symbolic of the mechanistic attitude behind man's new technology; its construction out of the parts of dead corpses is a logical extension of the reductive equation of living things with inorganic matter. The Monster as technological double parallels its function as dream self, giving form to the threatening attitude Mrs. Shelley saw behind much of modern science.

⌊While creating the Monster, Frankenstein forgets his family and friends and ignores the natural world. He also shuts off his own natural feelings of disgust. Only in retrospect can he remember,⌉

> ... the horrors of my secret toil, as I dabbled among the unhallowed damps of the grave, or tortured the living animal to animate the lifeless clay ... My limbs now tremble, and my eyes swim with the remembrance, but then a resistless, and almost frantic, impulse, urged me forward; I seemed to have lost all soul and sensation but for this one pursuit ... often did my human nature turn with loathing from my occupation, whilst, still urged on by an eagerness which perpetually increased, I brought my work near to a conclusion ... I wished, as it were, to procrastinate all that related to my feelings of affection until the great object, which swallowed up every habit of my nature, should be completed.

Simply put, Frankenstein, a classic megalomaniac, thinks "with mounting excitement that he has grasped and solved great cosmic riddles; he therefore loses all touch with reality. A reliable symptom of this condition is the loss of one's sense of humor and of human contacts." [9]

63

Too late, Frankenstein realizes that this detachment from human feeling has been the cause of much of the world's misery. He tells Walton, "if no man allowed any pursuit whatsoever to interfere with the tranquillity of his domestic affections, Greece had not been enslaved; Caesar would have spared his country; America would have been discovered more gradually; and the empires of Mexico and Peru had not been destroyed." This same dangerous sublimation of Frankenstein's "feelings of affection" determines the nature of his technology. Designed to be beautiful and loving, it is loathsome and unloved. It lives alone, far from the man and nature, venting its hatred on those its creator ignored. The libido Frankenstein poured into what he called his "child" has no outlet; deprived of human companionship, it explodes into violence. In trying to become the father of a new species, Frankenstein loses control of himself. Like the Faustian overreachers before him, his desire for preeminence only makes him preeminent in misery. But, with the power of the "new alchemy," the scale has changed. Earlier Fausts only threatened themselves; this technological double has more than human power and threatens to "make the very existence of the species of man a condition precarious and full of terror."

Frankenstein is the first modern science fiction novel, although Mrs. Shelley is less concerned with the hardware of science than with its implications.[10] We should remember that, like much science fiction, her novel is a projection into the immediate future of contemporary research. It is only because nineteenth-century scientists were wrong in equating electricity with "life energy" that her immediate concern for the future of the race was unfounded. But the fascination with creating life goes on. Once, when George Wald addressed a university audience, some students eagerly demanded that he discuss the possibility of creating an artificial being, giving little thought to the desirability of doing so. The technological challenge was all that mattered.[11] Such attitudes almost gave us the SST and may yet bring the Monster to life. An article in the March 5, 1973, issue of the *New York Times Magazine* by Willard Gaylen is entitled "The *Frankenstein* Myth Becomes a Reality: We have the Awful Knowledge to Make Exact Copies of Human Beings." The method for making these doubles is "cloning" — using as little as one cell from an organism to grow genetically identical duplicates in the laboratory. In an apt throwback to Galvani's experiments, the technique has already been tried successfully on frogs. Whether humans will be next depends upon the outcome of the struggle between power and ethics depicted in *Frankenstein*. But even if actual doubles are never created, the implications of Frankenstein's experiment are still evident. All of the things man makes are to some extent copies of himself. Like human beings, they can be good or evil, benevolent or destructive, attractive or repulsive. But they always will be something more than their creator's conscious intentions. The ambiguous nature of the machine has never been symbolized more effectively than by what has been called "Mary Shelley's finest invention" [12] — the Monster.

CHAPTER V

The Monster

> In the first stage, one deals with the persona, and above all with
> the shadow. The patient dreams of a repulsive individual who is
> always different but retains certain features throughout, and also
> shows certain traits resembling the dreamer. Eventually the time
> comes for the patient to understand that this individual is none
> other than himself, or rather his shadow, and this enables him to
> become fully aware of those aspects of his personality that he has
> refused to see ... One should of course, accept the shadow, but
> at the same time render it harmless.
>
> HENRI ELLENBERGER

AT THE CENTER of *Frankenstein* is the Monster's own story.
The "horrid thing" of Mary Shelley's dream, the "filthy mass
that moved and talked," has all the deliciously frightening
appeal of the decaying creatures of horror tales. But at the
same time it is the first of a new species — a robot, or more
specifically, an android, programmed to destroy all whom its
creator outwardly loves. Articulate, intelligent, and sensitive,
the Monster argues eloquently for its right to exist, all the
while murdering the innocent to punish the guilty and generally frightening the wits out of anyone it meets. If Victor
Frankenstein's frenzied discovery of the "new alchemy"
makes him the first mad scientist, the existence of the Monster
presents him with the first and most enduring symbol of
modern technology. It also poses a problem that is still with
us — what are we to do with our creations, especially when

they fail to live up to the promises of their creators? The Monster is, on the deepest and most personal level, a projection of Mary Shelley's feelings of isolation and hatred. On a larger scale it serves the same function. An orphan of science, created and abandoned, the Monster threatens to take out its anger and rejection on the species of man. Readers of *Frankenstein* have, from its first publication in 1818, had to face the Monster's arguments and decide if it has a right to survive or if, indeed, it is a monster at all.

In an early review of his wife's novel, Shelley argued that there is, in effect, no monster in *Frankenstein*. Like many later writers on the subject, he takes the creature at its word, asserting that its crimes are not "the offspring of any unaccountable propensity to evil, but flow irresistibly from certain causes fully adequate to their production. They are the children, as it were, of Necessity and Human Nature ... In this the direct moral of the book consists ... Treat a person wicked and he will become wicked." [1] Shelley's apologetics turn on the word "person." If the Monster is fully human, then mankind's treatment of it is criminal. But as self-projection, Doppelgänger, or infernal machine, it is clear that the Monster has the superhuman power and destructiveness of a creature of myth.

For one thing, it is abominable. The classic monsters of legend, like the Minotaur, Dragon, or Gorgon, grotesquely combine the characteristics of more than one animal. As a result, they stand outside of the normal categories of nature. The Monster is even more horrible. Half human, half machine, it falls somewhere between life and death, a thing so unnatural that any human it meets responds with an instinctive and overwhelming loathing. Even Walton, at the end of Frankenstein's long story, knowing what he will see, confronts the Monster and confesses that "I dared not again raise my eyes to his face, there was something so scaring and unearthly in his ugliness." This unearthliness, which makes human acceptance out of the question, is underscored by the Monster's namelessness. In Genesis 3:19–20, Adam's dominion over plants and animals is demonstrated by his power to name them; knowing the name of something has traditionally conferred magical control over it, as well as giving it a place in an ordered universe. Frankenstein's creation is simply "the Monster" — aptly communicating its total otherness and man's impotence before it.

The physical characteristics of the Monster are inherited from a whole family of humanoid monsters that stalk the world of folklore. As a girl growing up in England and Scotland, Mary Godwin no doubt heard some version of the series of legends of the monstrous offspring of Cain, of whom Grendel is the most familiar. She also probably heard the middle European folk tale of the Golem while on her travels and may even have met a "wild man" as part of a Swiss or Bavarian carnival or mummers play. This fur-covered creature, half man, half animal, was supposed to inhabit the forests and glaciers of Europe. As old as the *Gilgamesh* epic and Genesis (16:12), the story of the wild man is found in medieval art, legend, and literature. An outcast like our Monster, it was said to reach out from the darkness to attack the unwary. In the traditional ritual, which still survives, someone dressed as the wild man appears and causes mock terror among the villagers, who drive out, capture, or "kill" it; a similar episode occurs in *Frankenstein* and has become an obligatory scene in nearly all the Frankenstein films.[2] But more important than the Monster's genetic background is its moral ancestry. For this we must turn to a figure that, like Prometheus, was elevated to heroic status by many Romantic writers. For Blake and Shelley, Milton's Satan was an admirable rebel, a Prometheus gone wrong. For Mrs. Shelley, he was the monstrous double of Lucifer, Arch-angel turned Arch-destroyer, and his story a subtle argument from the Prince of Lies himself.

Paradise Lost (1667) is, like *Frankenstein*, designed to define man's place in the universe and give form to those forces threatening to displace him. Milton tells the apocryphal Christian myth of the Fall of the rebel angels and its effect upon human history. Lucifer, one of the most beautiful of the archangels, jealous of Christ's place in the Divine Family, revolts against his creator and tries to command heavenly power. For their crime he and his legion of followers are cast out of Heaven into Hell and transformed into the hideous Satan and his crew of devils. In the infernal Palace of Pandemonium, they discuss how best to carry on the fight and finally resolve to become the implacable foes of humanity. Satan travels to earth, tempts Adam and Eve from the Garden of Eden, and begins man's long and bloody history. The poem ends with the distant promise of the redemption of Adam's descendants through the sacrifice of God's Son. Although Mrs. Shelley's God was certainly not Milton's, they shared a feeling for a divinely created natural order. Direct evidence of her reading of *Paradise Lost* in both 1815 and 1816 is everywhere in *Frankenstein*, from the epigraph to the Monster's last speech. While her references to the poem may be contradictory in a few places, in general they are not haphazard borrowings. Mrs. Shelley found in *Paradise Lost* a pattern which could give form to her fears and mythic shape to her understanding of what technology threatened for the future.

While planning his experiment, Victor felt like Lucifer: "I trod heaven in my thoughts, now exulting in my powers, now burning with the idea of their effects." Like Lucifer before the Fall, Frankenstein before the Monster is in rebellion against his own creator, jealous of his place in his own family, experimenting with a technological imitation of the heavenly thunderbolt, and planning to invert the natural order of things. The interplay of Frankenstein/Monster is somewhat like the relationship between Lucifer/Satan. Each "monster" is, in outward appearance, a reflection of the inner self of its creator, both separate entity and other self, conceived at the moment of rebellion against God and given form when hoped-for triumph gives way to disaster. Thus, the most beautiful of archangels becomes his own monster, cast into Hell with only his memories and evil intact. Similarly, at the moment the Monster comes to life, Frankenstein remembers:

> His limbs were in proportion, and I had selected his features as beautiful. Beautiful! — Great God! His yellow skin scarcely covered the work of muscles and arteries beneath; his hair was of a lustrous black, and flowing; his teeth of a pearly whiteness; but these luxuriances only formed a more horrid contrast with his watery eyes . . . shrivelled complexion and straight black lips . . . the beauty of the dream vanished, and breathless horror and disgust filled my heart.

The transformation of beautiful dream to loathsome reality begins Frankenstein's long fall to isolation and death. At the end of his life, he realizes the epic dimensions of his crime and its punishment: ". . . like the archangel who aspired to omnipotence, I am chained in an eternal hell."

At first, Frankenstein tries to escape his chains. He runs from his creation in terror and, for a time, believes he is free. But, on the icy slopes of Chamounix glacier, he meets it again and hears its story. The Monster documents its slow transformation from would-be new Adam, to fallen angel, to modern Satan as a painful self-awakening. It begins its independent life without history — part child, part man, part machine. Only with time will it learn that all of man's world is a garden from which it is excluded, that Nature itself has no place for it, and that its only universe is Milton's "universe of death" — the Hell that is always around it.

Its first days in a forest near Ingolstadt resemble what was, at the time, considered the ideal condition for man — the state of nature. Jean Jacques Rousseau argued in his writings that civilization was a corrupting influence and that man, in his "natural state," was "an animal less strong than some, and less agile than others, but, upon the whole, the most advantageously organized of any; I see him satisfying his hunger under an oak, and his thirst at the first brook; I see him laying himself down to sleep at the foot of the same tree that afforded him his meal and there all his wants completely supplied." [3] This snug vision of the past assumed that all men were at peace, amply supplied with food and shelter and able to learn speech by imitating animal sounds.[4] If Rousseau had been looking, he would have seen the Monster beginning his life in exactly this way — living on acorns, nuts, and berries, drinking from a brook, and sleeping under a tree. Unfortunately, nothing works. It fails to find enough food or adequate shelter; when it tries to imitate the birds' songs, the horrid grunts that emerge frighten it into silence. Its inability to live in what was thought to be the most natural state for man points up its unnaturalness — the world of Nature is hostile to a being that doesn't fit. The landscape the Monster finds himself in is more like the vast wasteland Satan and his legions discover when they awaken from the shock of their own fall into damnation.

The "burning lake" of *Paradise Lost* lies in a "frozen Continent," "dark and wild, beat with perpetual storms" [5] where the fallen angels are punished by being made to feel "fierce extremes by change more fierce / From beds of raging Fire to starve in Ice." [6] Hopeless, lost, and confused, the beaten army

> Viewed first their lamentable lot, and found
> No rest: through many a dark and dreary Vale
> They pass'd, and many a Region dolorous
> O'er many a frozen, many a fiery Alp,
> Rocks, Caves, Lakes, Fens, Bogs, and shades of death.[7]

These waste places have their traditional monstrous inhabitants:

> ... Nature breeds,
> Perverse, all monstrous, all prodigious things,
> Abominable, inutterable, and worse
> Than fables yet have feign'd, or fear conceived.[8]

Clearly, Rousseau's state of Nature is, for the Monster, a Miltonic place of infernal torment. Its first sensations are of the painful alteration of light and dark; it remembers "feeling pain invade me from all sides." Extremes of cold and heat continue to oppress the Monster; half-frozen, it discovers a fire and innocently puts its hand in the embers, with predictable results. Throughout its unnatural existence, the Monster remains in an icy "universe of death" beyond the boundaries of the living world — a place Milton describes as fit for monsters. Yet it is always also associated with fire and lightning. For example, it first appears to Frankenstein after the creation in a flash of lightning that illuminates "the lake, making it appear like a vast sheet of fire," while it ultimately chooses fire as its instrument of self-destruction. But, at the start of its existence, it is unaware of where it is, and what it will become. Wandering in its cold world, it finds its first refuge in a hut abandoned by a shepherd, a place it later calls "as exquisite and divine a retreat as Pendaemonium [*sic*] appeared to the daemons of hell after their sufferings in the lake of fire."

In *Paradise Lost*, after the meeting in Pandemonium, Satan decides to fly to earth to inspect God's latest creation. Taking the form of a cormorant, he perches on a tree in Eden and secretly observes Adam and Eve in the Garden. Their happiness reminds him of his eternal pain, and ultimately he finds the way to tempt them to sin. After the Monster has left the shepherd's hut, traveled to a village, and been driven out in a hail of stones, it hides in a hovel where it can secretly observe the lives of a noble family reduced to poverty. Here, it learns man's language, history, and its own true nature. The episode follows the Miltonic pattern; hidden in this new Eden, the Monster learns its Satanic role as the destroyer of human happiness.

While it was traditional at the time to romanticize the lives of the rural poor, to the Monster's eyes, the world it sees is more than romantic — it is "indeed a Paradise." It first observes a man and woman, Felix and Agatha De Lacey, working in the fields. Although the De Laceys have fallen on hard times, from the Monster's viewpoint they live in a perfect environment: "They possessed a delightful house (for such it was in my eyes) and every luxury; they had a fire to warm them when chill, and delicious viands when hungry; they were dressed in excellent clothes; and, still more, they enjoyed one another's company and speech." The weather, in contrast to the cold and damp of the Monster's first days, is magical: "[Rain] frequently took place; but a high wind quickly dried the earth, and the season became far more pleasant than it had been." The cottage is even surrounded by a garden, where their blind father (God?) walks every day, and which is Felix's job to cultivate.

The Monster frequently peers in the window and watches the son and daughter listen to their father play the violin. It remembers being filled with "a mixture of pain and pleasure, such as I had never before experienced . . . I withdrew from the window, unable to bear these emotions." Satan feels a similar torment as he spies on Adam and Eve:

> Imparadis't in one another's arms . . . while I to
>   Hell am thrust,
> Where neither joy nor love, but fierce desire
> Among our other torments not the least
> Still unfulfilled with pain of longing pines.[9]

The difference, of course, is that Satan knows he is a devil, condemned to Hell forever, while the Monster still believes it can find a place in the world of man and nature, even though the old man's violin makes sounds "sweeter than the thrush or nightingale" while its own attempts at imitating the birds frighten it into silence. Though it looks vaguely like a man, the Monster slowly discovers the great gulf between itself and all things human. It recalls, "I had admired the perfect forms of my cottagers — their grace, beauty, and delicate complexions; but how was I terrified when I viewed myself in a transparent pool! At first I started back, unable to believe that it was indeed I who was reflected in the mirror; and when I became fully convinced that I was in reality the monster that I am, I was filled with the bitterest sensations of despondence and mortification. Alas! I did not yet entirely know the fatal effects of this miserable deformity." The Monster, at this time only able to form its concepts from those around it, looks at the reflection as if it were a man looking at some hideous thing. It is yet to find a model for the totality of its being.

The Monster does have one remarkable stroke of luck: it manages to learn much of human history, as well as how to read and speak, by eavesdropping on Felix, who is conveniently teaching French from a history book to an Arabian girl. Unlikely as it might be, the episode does explain the Monster's literacy, as well as introduce it to the long history of human evil and duplicity. It also leads the Monster to ask itself,

> And what was I? Of my creation and creator I was absolutely ignorant, but I knew that I possessed no money, no friends, no kind of property. I was, besides, endued with a figure hideously deformed and loathsome; I was not even of the same nature as man. I was more agile than they, and could subsist upon coarser diet; I bore the extremes of heat and cold with less injury to my frame; my stature far exceeded theirs. When I looked around, I saw and heard of none like me. Was I then a monster, a blot upon the earth, from which all men fled, and whom all men disowned?

The recitation of man's history and culture has taught the Monster the extent of its isolation; nowhere in the world of men does it find a counterpart.

The Monster soon stumbles upon three books: *Paradise Lost*, a volume of Plutarch's *Lives*, and Goethe's *Sorrows of Werter* [sic]. In the hero of *Werter* it sees "a more divine being than I ever beheld or imagined," but the novel leads it again to notice how "I found myself similar, yet at the same time strangely unlike to the beings concerning whom I read . . . Who was I? What was I?" In Plutarch it finds "high thoughts" but no answer to its question. But *Paradise Lost*, which it reads as a "true history," contains the solution:

> I often referred the several situations, as their similarity struck me to my own. Like Adam, I was apparently united by no link to any other being in existence; but his state was far different from mine in every other respect. He had come forth from the hands of God a perfect creature, happy and prosperous, guarded by the especial care of his Creator . . . but I was wretched, helpless, and alone. Many times I considered Satan as the fitter emblem of my condition; for often, like him, when I viewed the bliss of my protectors, the bitter gall of envy rose within me.

Milton, therefore, provides the Monster with an identity. Although not yet rejected by the De Laceys, it recognizes that, like Satan, the happiness of men only goads it to evil. From this moment on, the Monster begins to wear the Satanic cloak it has found. It finds some papers in its pockets, reads of its human creation, yet still uses Milton's metaphor: "Satan had his companions, fellow-devils, to admire and encourage him; but I am solitary and abhorred." However, the Monster still dreams of Paradise and makes one last attempt to enter its gates.

It has been leaving an appropriate gift at the De Laceys door each morning — a pile of firewood. One day it enters the cottage when only the blind old man is there and attempts to win his sympathy. It still half believes that it is a monster only in appearance, that "a fatal prejudice clouds [men's] eyes, and where they ought to see a feeling and kind friend, they behold only a detestable monster." The old man listens and replies, "it will afford me true pleasure to be in any way serviceable to a *human* creature" (author's italics). When the family returns, the Monster is, of course, chased out as the old man, sensing its inhuman nature, asks "Great God! ... Who are you?" The Monster has learned; its abominable nature cannot be embraced by the old man's sympathy for all things human.

The Monster's response to this rejection, which also drives the De Lacey family from their Eden, is a final confirmation of its Satanic nature. In *Paradise Lost* Satan ends the Council in Hell by vowing to revenge himself upon God by finding a way to destroy God's favored species,

> By sudden onset, either with Hell fire
> To waste his whole Creation, or possess
> All as our own, and drive as we were driven,
> The puny habitants, or if not drive,
> Seduce them to our party.[10]

The Monster's first reaction to rejection is to feel "rage and revenge. I could with pleasure have destroyed the cottage and its inhabitants, and have glutted myself with their shrieks and misery." It declares: "I, like the arch-fiend, bore a hell within me; and, finding myself unsympathized with, wished to tear up the trees, spread havoc and destruction around me, and then to have sat down and enjoyed the ruin ... from that moment I declared everlasting war against the species, and, more than all, against him who had formed me, and sent me forth to this insupportable misery." The Monster's response to his rejection is finally to give vent to a cosmic, unchecked, and Satanic fury: "... unable to injure any thing human, I turned my fury towards inanimate objects ... [I] destroyed every vestige of cultivation in the garden ... As the night advanced, a fierce wind arose from the woods, and quickly dispersed the clouds that had loitered in the heavens: the blast tore along like a mighty avalanche, and produced a kind of insanity in my spirits, that burst all bounds of reason and reflection." In its fury, the Monster burns down the cabin and heads out to the Hell of the frozen Continent: "Nature decayed around me, and the sun became heatless; rain and snow poured around me; mighty rivers were frozen; the surface of the earth was hard and chill, and bare, and I found no shelter ... The mildness of my nature had fled, and all within me was turned to gall and bitterness."

The Monster returns to its cold Hell, confirmed in its evil. It goes on systematically to murder Frankenstein's family and friends, strangling his young brother, William, with "exultation and hellish triumph," causing the death of his "step-servant," Justine, his best friend, Henry Clerval, and his bride, Elizabeth. At the beginning of its story, the Monster tells Frankenstein, "I ought to be thy Adam; but I am rather the fallen angel, whom thou drivest from joy for no misdeed. Every where I see bliss, from which I alone am irrevocably excluded." At the end, it realizes that "the fallen angel becomes a malignant devil." The Monster's agony as the hideous product of a scientist's flawed vision gives it no place to turn but to Satan for a mirror. The goal of its existence becomes the damnation of its Maker, as it lures Frankenstein to its own isolated Hell on the ice fields of the Arctic. The Monster's crimes, like its isolation, are irrevocably determined by Frankenstein's crime of giving awareness to a thing that can never find a place in the world of man and nature. Therefore the importance of Milton's epigraph

> Did I request thee, Maker, from my clay
> To mould me Man? Did I solicit thee
> From darkness to promote me? — [11]

77

In Milton's poem, Adam asks this of his God; in Mrs. Shelley's novel, Frankenstein's would-be Adam asks it of man. Once given life, the products of an unnatural technology can never fit into the natural world and, in Mrs. Shelley's view, must inevitably come to oppose it. Their methods are Satan's — either direct destruction or the "seduction" of man to their side. Thus the danger inherent in the Monster's eloquent, persuasive, but diabolical arguments for its own survival.

When the Monster finishes its tale, it asks its creator to build it a mate, promising they will go off together to the "wilds of South America" and never bother mankind again. But, Frankenstein has learned the lesson of the Monster's story. In the Council in Hell in *Paradise Lost*, one of the devils, Mammon, argues like the Monster that the devils should abandon their fight against God and build a separate, isolated kingdom. But Beelzebub, supporting Satan, replies that it is the devils' unalterable nature to oppose God. Frankenstein similarly replies, "How long can you, who long for the love and sympathy of man, persevere in this exile? You will return, and again seek their kindness, and you will meet with their detestation; your evil passions will be renewed, and you will then have a companion to aid you in the task of destruction." Frankenstein also fears the Monster's Satanic guile: "May not even this be a feint that will increase your triumph by affording a wider scope for revenge?" He is nevertheless almost convinced but destroys the Monster's bride-to-be at the last moment, realizing that by allowing the products of technology to proliferate he will only increase the danger to mankind: "one of the first results of those sympathies for which the daemon thirsted would be children, and a race of devils would be propagated on earth, who might make the very species of man a condition precarious and full of terror."

He ignores the obvious solution — as creator, he could surely leave out a part or two to insure foolproof birth control. But the assumption that they will be fertile helps the technological prophecy. The "new species" created to "bless man" has become a potential race of devils plotting to make the human species extinct. Like any living thing, man's creations will cling to life; their lives must, however, ultimately thrive at the expense of their creators, since both cannot share the same world. Technology need not threaten us by a sudden assault on our world. Instead, it can slowly build its own empire, propagate a "race of devils," and transform earth into a Hell suitable for its existence. At the time Mrs. Shelley worked on *Frankenstein*, what Blake called the "dark Satanic Mills" of the Industrial Revolution were pouring an inferno of smoke and fire over the English landscape and subjecting workers to the relentless rhythm of the machine. Byron's maiden speech in the House of Lords, on February 27, 1812, concerned the mobs of displaced laborers who were threatened by Parliament with execution for wrecking the new machinery. It may indeed have seemed that the old world was crumbling and a new kingdom was taking shape.

At the end of *Paradise Lost*, Adam is given a vision of man's future history; he learns that eventually his suffering will end and that, through Christ, he will come to know Paradise again. *Frankenstein* has no such optimistic vision, though it does hold out some hope for a more rational science. The tale told to Walton is a warning — made clear by Frankenstein's final assessment of his treatment of the Monster:

> During these last days I have been occupied in examining my past conduct; nor do I find it blameable. In a fit of enthusiastic madness I created a rational creature and was bound towards him, to assure, as far as was in my power, his happiness and well-being. That was my duty; but there was another still paramount to that. My duties towards the beings of my own species had greater claims to my attention, because they included a greater proportion of happiness or misery. Urged

by this view, I refused, and I did right in refusing, to create a companion for the first creature. He showed unparalleled malignity and selfishness, in evil: he destroyed my friends; he devoted to destruction beings who possessed exquisite sensations, happiness, and wisdom; nor do I know where this thirst for vengeance may end. Miserable himself, that he might render no other wretched, he ought to die."

Frankenstein asks Walton to destroy the Monster, warning him of its Satanic nature: The Monster "is eloquent and persuasive; and once his words had even power over my heart; but trust him not. His soul is as hellish as his form, full of treachery and fiendlike malice." The Monster tells Walton that it was the "slave, not the master of an impulse which I detested, yet could not disobey" and that its murders tortured its heart, even while it was committing them." We are reminded of its subservience to Frankenstein's unconscious wishes, as well as Satan's lament,

> Ay, me, they little know
> How dearly I abide that boast so vain
> Under what torments I inwardly groan
> While they adore me on the Throne of Hell
> The lower still I fall, Only Supreme
> In misery.[12]

The truth is contained in an even closer paraphrase of Milton, when the Monster admits to Walton that "evil thenceforth became my good ... The completion of my demonical design became an insatiable passion."

Walton at first feels pity, but then, looking at the corpse of his only friend, sees the true face of the Monster. He calls it a "hypocritical fiend," realizing "if he whom you mourn still lived, still would he be the object, again would he become the prey, of your accursed vengeance. It is not pity that you feel; you lament only because the victim of your malignity is with-

drawn from your power." The last human being it meets
spurns the Monster, with reason. Walton knows that the im-
possibility of man's acceptance only drives the Monster to
"hellish malice," just as the exclusion of Satan from God's love
leads him to further damn himself. As a symbol for a demonic
technology, the Monster never loses the pathetic quality of an
abandoned child that strikes out at a world it can never join.
Throughout the Monster's story, the human and natural world
was a kind of Paradise from which it alone was excluded.
When it decides to travel to the North Pole, the farthest point
from all of humanity, and there somehow find enough wood
to build its funeral pyre, it seeks the culmination of its Satanic
identity. Mrs. Shelley was reading Dante while working on
Frankenstein and, at the bottom of his Hell, at the greatest
distance from God, she found Lucifer, locked in ice.
The Monster's vision of its own destruction, in the center of
a frozen landscape, "exult[ing] in the agony of the torturing
flames," brings together the images of cold and fire that accompanied it since its first awakening and finally gives the
Monster a place in the mythological cosmos it can call its
own.

Born of Frankenstein's megalomania, the Monster through
its growing awareness of its identity defines the dimensions of
its maker's dangerous madness and ties together the many
threads of Mary Shelley's novel. Linked in life and death,
Frankenstein and Monster are separate entities and one being,
a Lucifer/Satan who play out the Romantic closet drama of
the mind, the myth of self-exploration and self-awareness, on
a stage that spans the terra incognita of space and time, the unexplored Arctic, and the unexperienced future. The power of
technology gives Frankenstein's dream self a concrete reality
and a separate existence, allowing it to act out its maker's fantasies with terrible results. That it becomes a devil is deter-

mined by the nature of Frankenstein's experiment and his blindness to his own motivations. Both creator and creature are presented to Walton as an object lesson, a warning of where a narcissistic science can lead.[13]

The end of the novel is ambiguous. Frankenstein has been led to the Arctic wastes by his Monster and dies with nothing but his dreams to sustain him. Although he has reminded Walton of his paramount duties toward his fellow man, Frankenstein's last words betray his ignorance of the meaning of his own destruction: "Seek happiness in tranquillity, and avoid ambition, even if it be only the apparently innocent one of distinguishing yourself in science and discoveries. Yet why do I say this? I have myself been blasted in these hopes, yet another may succeed." Walton only turns his ship around at the instigation of his crew, feeling "ignorant and disappointed" and condemning their "cowardice and indecision." But he has learned that his explorations must begin with true concern for his fellow man. Rather than sacrificing human life to his own desire for knowledge and power, he realizes that he cannot lead his crew "unwillingly to danger," that ". . . it is terrible to reflect that the lives of all these men are endangered through me. If we are lost, my mad schemes are the cause."

Mrs. Shelley leaves Walton on the Polar Sea, heading south, toward the rest of the human race. He has met the Monster and cast it back into the darkness, having seen the demonic results of isolation and monomania. At the start of his journey he believed he could escape his own self through scientific exploration, comparing his feelings as he set out to "the joy a child feels when he embarks in a little boat, with his holiday mates, on an expedition of discovery up his native river." Through Frankenstein's parallel tale, he discovers where that "native river" actually leads — "to the forgotten sources" of the "mountain river" of his past. The insight of *Frankenstein* is that awareness of the self and hope for the future of humanity are inextricably bound together.

In Canto XXXI of the *Inferno*, Dante is shown the Titans, who struggled against God, at the edge of the frozen pool of Cocytus, in the last circle of Hell. Although not mentioned in the poem, Prometheus, a Titan, presumably would be found there as well. When Walton watches Frankenstein waste away from cold and deprivation on his icebound ship he, like Dante, witnesses the terrible punishment extracted for the crime of pride and rebellion against the natural order. Both travelers journey past suffering to a greater understanding of themselves and the universe. In the fourteenth century, Hell awaited the sinner after death; at the start of the Industrial Revolution, a new Inferno threatened to engulf the future of mankind. The message Walton brings back from the Arctic is directed to "Mrs. Saville" and the modern world, and meant, like Dante's poem, to show the way to salvation. If man is to be saved he must join Mary Shelley in seeking a path out of what she once called "the icy region this heart encircles."

CHAPTER VI

Re-creation

Oh Horror! — let me fly this dreadful monster of my own creation!

Frankenstein, or the Man and the Monster! (1826)

The brain you stole, Fritz. Think of it! The brain of a dead man waiting to live again in a body I made with my own hands!

Frankenstein (1931)

"Alone you have created a man. Now, together, we will create his mate."
   "You mean...?"
   "Yes! A woman! That should be really interesting!"

The Bride of Frankenstein (1935)

MARY SHELLEY's nightmare-turned-novel was a success almost from the day it was published and ultimately became one of the most popular books ever written. The story of Frankenstein and his Monster became a part of our culture, emerging in the next century and a half in various guises. It influenced *Moby Dick, Wuthering Heights,* and *Dr. Jekyll and Mr. Hyde,* as well as literally hundreds of science fiction short stories, beginning with Melville's "The Bell Tower" in 1847. Many plays purporting to be based upon the novel brought an echo of Mary Shelley's vision to the theater. The author herself attended the first production, Richard Brinsley Peake's *Pre-sumption, or the Fate of Frankenstein*, at the English Opera House in 1823. Although almost all of these melodramas are forgettable in themselves, they are necessary steps in the evolution of the Frankenstein myth, linking the novel with the films that have kept the story before a mass audience throughout the twentieth century.

〈 In the many stage versions, the complexities of the novel were reduced to a few spectacular scenes — the creation, destruction of the De Lacey cottage, and death of the Monster were perennial favorites. (Peake even alternated the catastrophes with irrelevant songs, unintentionally creating the first musical comedy production.) The novel, after all, travels all over the map and keeps much of the action at secondhand or within the minds of the characters. Playwrights had to emphasize the dramatic and sensational in order to suit the taste of nineteenth-century audiences for melodrama. As a result, they returned to the "monstrous engine" and "horrid thing" of Mrs. Shelley's dream. The Monster became mute, given to crashing through doors and otherwise displaying its brute power. The same two actors, Thomas Potter Cooke and Richard John ("O.") Smith, performed the role in play after play. Much of the action, including the creation scene, soon became stylized, though each production tried to outdo the last in staging the Monster's death. It was buried in an avalanche, jumped into the smoking crater of a volcano, froze in an Arctic storm, and burned to death in a church. Excess soon gave way to parody; a series of short-lived burlesques aped the Frankenstein stage tradition.[2] This same formula became familiar to a new audience when the story was retold in the twentieth century through the technological medium of the motion picture. Film is perfect for sustaining myth. Each moviegoer is isolated in the darkness, seeing his fantasies projected before him while, at the same time, he is bound to those around him by the similarities in culture that produce popular film. For the Frankenstein myth, film is itself evidence of Mary Shelley's prophecy come true — the culmination of what Professor Waldman called the power to "mock the invisible world with its own shadows." Alone together at the movies, we experience the fusion of self, society, and technology that is the domain of the myth of Frankenstein.

The story first came to the screen in two silents, the Edison Company version (1910) and *Life Without Soul* (1915). The Edison *Frankenstein*, starring Charles Ogle as a barrel-chested, Brillo-haired Monster, was only one reel long and consisted of twenty-five hand-tinted scenes of the Monster's creation and destruction. A transitional piece, it retained the structure of the melodramas while demonstrating the additional effects possible with film. It is of interest chiefly because of its conclusion — in a bow to the Doppelgänger tradition and a demonstration of the power of cinema, the Monster fades away before a mirror, leaving its reflection behind. As Frankenstein embraces his bride, the reflection disappears, showing the relationship between the "domestic affections" of the scientist and the existence of the creature — a recurring theme. *Life Without Soul*, four reels longer, is notable for its far-flung locales, its un-made-up Monster, and the sympathy Percy Darrell Standing evoked in his role as "The Creation." But both these films are lost; the 1931 version, directed by James Whale and starring Colin Clive, May Clarke, and Boris Karloff, really reanimates the Frankenstein myth for the twentieth century and remains the most famous horror film ever made.

Frankenstein was originally envisioned as a companion piece to Universal's *Dracula* (1931). That film ends with Edward Van Sloan coming from behind a curtain to argue the existence of vampires; he returns before the opening credits of *Frankenstein* to warn us of the ensuing threat to our nerves.

He and Dwight Frye play similar roles in both films. His Professor Waldman is really a Professor Van Helsing who tries,
but fails, to destroy the Monster, while the words Frye made
famous as Dracula's mad disciple Renfield — a whispered "Yes,
Master" — have become part of the vocabulary of laboratory
assistants, though they are never spoken in *Frankenstein.* Both
films have, as their immediate inspiration, stage plays and
not the novels. This source almost proves fatal for *Dracula,*
which too often bogs down in talkiness. The theatrical roots
of *Frankenstein* (primarily a play by Peggy Webling, adapted
by William Hurlbut and John Balderston) are responsible
for some of the more static moments in that film, as well as the
name changes (Victor becomes Henry, Henry Clerval becomes Victor Moritz) and the famous scene between the
Monster and the little girl. Robert Florey, who was first slated
to direct the film, contributed its most absurd and unnecessary
sequence, when Fritz, Frankenstein's assistant, mistakenly
steals a pickled criminal brain (prominently labeled "AB-
NORMAL BRAIN," "DISFUNCTIO CEREBRI") from Goldstadt Medical College.[3]

However, Florey may have had something to do with the
marvelous sets, designed by Charles D. Hall and Herman
Rosse, which brought German expressionism to the American
film. Frankenstein's watchtower-laboratory is a jumbled collection of massive, off-plumb walls, crazily tilted beams, and
oddly cut windows — there seems not to be one right angle
in the place. The inspiration is no doubt films like Robert
Weine's classic *The Cabinet of Dr. Caligari* (1919) and Paul
Wegener's *The Golem* (1920). *Caligari* is a relevant Gothic
parable of an authoritarian doctor's power over a young man
who is both his instrument and victim — the somnambulist
Cesare. The setting is a surreal landscape which gives the
scenes the fragile and threatening perspective of nightmare.
The Golem uses the same methods in a more muted fashion,

87

retelling the medieval monster legend in a gnarled Prague ghetto that seems about to collapse at any moment. Florey's original conception of the Monster was clearly modeled closely on Wegener's most famous role. Some test scenes were even shot with Bela Lugosi stomping around the set of Dracula's castle in Golem make-up.

The convoluted genesis of the film could well have destroyed it. But Robert Florey was relieved of his directoral duties and replaced by James Whale, who was responsible for casting Colin Clive as Frankenstein and, when Lugosi rejected the Monster role, recruiting an obscure English actor, William Henry Pratt, who, in 1910, had taken the stage name Boris Karloff. He also brought to the production a distinctive style and organizing vision. Retaining an expressionist feel for light and shape, he expanded the dimensions of space and movement, giving *Frankenstein* a feeling of openness that *Dracula* lacks. Whale explored the conflicts at the core of the myth while contributing his own interest in the humanity of monsters and the inhumanity of man. The result is a *Frankenstein* with new relevance for a world recovering from the Great War, in the depths of the Depression, and threatened with a more terrifying conflict in the future.

The time of the film is indefinite but appears to be contemporary; the place has moved from the cities of Geneva and Ingolstadt to a remote village somewhere in central Europe. Victor Frankenstein created his Monster in the bare attic room of a boarding house in the midst of a thriving city; his curse as the novel progresses is his gradual estrangement from humanity. Henry Frankenstein chooses to isolate himself in an old watchtower in a blasted, empty landscape, far from humanity and its needs. James Whale was British, served in World War I, and grew thin in a German prison camp. He made his reputation directing the sardonic war drama *Journey's End* on stage and as a film. R. C. Sherriff's play is set in the trenches; Whale's film has the distinct atmosphere of No Man's Land — intensified by the opening scenes of graveyards, gibbets, and corpses. The technological horror that Mrs. Shelley feared seemed to have arrived in the "war to end all wars" — a conflict which only succeeded in destroying a generation and destroying belief in progress and the nobility of man. Whale retells the myth after disaster has come; the nameless forces which brought about the war and Depression are, in his film, tinkering among the ruins with new and greater powers, threatening to unleash an even more spectacular disaster.

The laboratory in the ruined watchtower, the most famous set in all Frankenstein films, evokes the attraction and repulsion science holds for the layman. The central structure is a glittering gadget (designed by Kenneth Strickfaden) that hauls the Monster through a skylight into the midst of an electrical storm, where it receives the mysterious spark of life from "the great ray that first brought life into the world." The crescendo of effects that brings the Monster to life is the scene we all remember first from the film — a controlled catastrophe combining our fascination for electronic wizardry with the horror of its product. The capture of nature's lightning inside the tower suggests, as it does in the novel, the Promethean travesty of cosmic power put in mortal hands. As the fingers of the creature move, Frankenstein maniacally shouts, over and over, "IT'S ALIVE!" until he has to be restrained. When Victor Moritz admonishes, "Henry, in the name of God!" he replies, "Oh — in the name of God. Now I know what it feels like to *be* God!" Although this bit of megalomania was cut from some later prints of the film, the madness of the whole project is quite evident. In Mary Shelley's novel, the interplay between the characters takes place in the external world and within one mind. The failure of Frankenstein's experiment is due to his ignorance of the contradictory possibilities within his own personality. In much the same way, the laboratory scenes in the film both caricature modern technology, laboring in electrical splendor to bring forth a monstrosity, and define the relationship between the Monster and the mind of Henry Frankenstein.

This aspect of the laboratory becomes clearer when we look at a character derived from the plays but given his own prominence in the film. Frankenstein's hunchback assistant, played with demonic glee by Dwight Frye, joins Frankenstein on his midnight rambles to the gibbet and graveyard and guards the door of the watchtower. He is responsible for the "criminal brain" (a cumbersome attempt at establishing motivation) and amuses himself by torturing the newly resurrected Monster with whips, chains, and torches until it responds by hanging him. No doubt, Fritz is descended from the imps and demons who accompanied medieval sorcerers, as well as the stock comic assistant of melodrama (the servant in *Presumption*, the first *Frankenstein* play, is even named Fritz) with a cinematic bow to *Dracula's* Renfield and Lon Chaney's Quasimodo from the 1923 version of *The Hunchback of Notre Dame*. But Whale gives him a personality all his own. He is afraid of the electrical storm and the unawakened Monster. In one memorable scene, like the porter in *Macbeth*,[4] he answers the door, mumbling about "people messing about at this time of night" then stops to straighten his sock; in another, his twisted body clashes, physically and symbolically, with a hanging skeleton. Whale and Frye make Fritz an endearing, somewhat comic character. But he cannot be seen apart from his master; he may be the most grotesque incarnation of a standard American figure — the sidekick. Like Hawkeye and Chingachgook, Huck Finn and Jim or at a later date Matt Dillon and Chester, Frankenstein and Fritz face the future together, partners on a scientific frontier.

At the same time, since Fritz is so intimately involved with giving the Monster its destructive personality (via both the wrong brain and the wrong treatment), it is more than possible that he is a projection of the demon hidden in the mind of Henry Frankenstein — an embodiment of his twisted emotions. Fritz is first seen peering through a graveyard fence — the opening line in the film is Frankenstein hissing "Down . . . down, you fool!" Later we see him looking through the window at the Medical College and the grated door of the watchtower. He is the part of Frankenstein who must constantly be kept in check but always threatens to break out. The tower they share is itself symbolic of the mind. Isolated, rickety, yet topped by a gleaming laboratory, it embodies the aloofness, instability, and brilliance of its most famous tenant. But Fritz lives there too. He helps build the Monster and adjust the equipment, although his fears and sadistic pleasures imperil the experiment and ultimately sabotage it. While Fritz is tormenting the Monster with a torch, Frankenstein enters and ineffectually pleads, "Oh come away, Fritz. Just leave it alone. Leave it alone." Even though he has defied God, Fritz defies him. When the Monster finally hangs the hunchback, Frankenstein collapses on the stairs. Waldman must bring him to his senses with the telling line, "Come, come, pull yourself together!" He weakly replies, "What can we do?" and agrees to destroy the Monster. Soon after, he collapses again, moaning over and over, "Oh, my poor Fritz," then follows Waldman's suggestion to "Leave it all to me." The loss of Fritz, and his replacement by Waldman, suggest Frankenstein's change in moral direction. Throughout the experiment, he never seemed to realize that the Monster would be a product of himself and the hunchback — intellect served by demented feelings.

The Monster itself is both a pathetic creature — wandering, friendless, misunderstood — and a destructive menace. Boris Karloff's masterful portrayal, aided by Jack Pierce's equally masterful make-up job, created a Monster that was both abominable and sympathetic. Machinelike attributes (primarily a lurching walk and stiff movements) contrast with childlike innocence and a superhuman rage and power. Whale made the Monster's first appearance a study in its contradictions. We do not see it rise from the table. Instead, a few days later, Waldman and Frankenstein, sitting in a room in the tower, hear the Monster's heavy footsteps on the stairs. The first shot of the Monster, as it enters the darkened room, is from the back. It slowly turns and, in a series of quick cuts, Whale moves in to the face. Familiarity had not yet dimmed the shock of Karloff's cadaverous skull, circled by scars and pierced by clips and electrodes. It remains one of the most frightening moments in the history of film. This effective bit of horror is immediately followed by the opening of a shutter allowing light into the room. Like a child, the Monster raises its great hands, trying to catch the sunlight, while making an almost infantile mewling. We are left unsure what to feel, caught between the horror of its appearance and the appeal of its innocence. Its very innocence proves, in fact, to be dangerous. It drowns a little girl because it thinks she will float like the flowers the two have been throwing in the water. (This scene, incidentally, was cut in American prints at the insistence of Karloff, who later said that Whale had him throwing the girl in the water with too much violence, spoiling the sensitivity of the scene. As shown, we see the Monster reach for the girl, then cut to the girl's father carrying her corpse through the village. Unfortunately, the effect is much worse; anything but sensitivity is implied.) The Monster's only other murders are motivated by self-preservation. It strangles Waldman as the doctor is about to dissect it and hangs Fritz to end his torments. The shorthand of cinema precludes the philosophical complexities of Mrs. Shelley's Monster, but Karloff's creature draws its power from the same source — a carefully maintained balance between sympathy and horror.

The Monster as outcast also has contemporary political overtones. In one sense, it is a creature of the thirties, shaped by shadowy forces beyond its control, wandering the countryside like some disfigured veteran or hideous tramp. The special pathos of the Monster, never really recaptured in most of the later films, is due in part to its affinities with the refugees from political and economic disaster cast out from a society that can find no place for them. In many ways, the 1931 *Frankenstein* plays upon the particular collection of fears that haunted the thirties. The scientist and hunchback personify the forces of mad authority and sadistic servitude that brought disaster to the world and, perhaps, were plotting new horrors for the future. Their "science" is both technological and political; the Monster is weapon and victim, a mechanical engine of destruction and a collection of misused human beings. Its rage and rejection threaten all of society. At the same time, the film plays upon the seduction of gadgetry (our affinities with the scientist) and our identification with the isolation and sexual force of the Monster.

Whale's *Frankenstein* has its shortcomings; most are relics of its checkered origins. But Colin Clive does overact badly in spots and, for some reason, plays the last scenes in riding boots. The romantic interludes are pedestrian, while the comic old Baron seems dragged in for no purpose whatsoever. Whale used the most conventional methods for sequences which we may assume held no interest for him. He is best at "building" shots with careful framing, dramatic lighting, and a camera tilted slightly upward to suggest the monumentality of the figures. Whale's distinctive style comes, as well, from the inventive touches he added to what could have become stock situations. His grotesques — Fritz and the Monster — have the depth supplied by the director's attention to detail, while Elizabeth, the Baron, and Victor Moritz are cut from thin cardboard.

Although strongly influenced by expressionist cinematic techniques and led by his own taste for the unusual, Whale was familiar with Mary Shelley's novel. He carefully re-created the moment that Frankenstein finds Elizabeth's body sprawled on the bed, with the Monster peering through the window, although in this case she has only fainted. He also blended a pattern from the novel with his own ironic sym-bolism, creating two threads that wind through the film and come together in the last scenes. In the first minute of the film, a gravedigger pauses from his work to light his pipe. He thereby introduces the image of fire, which becomes, as it did in the novel, a metaphor for knowledge, power, and de-struction. As Fritz and Frankenstein enter the graveyard to dig up the body, the second motif becomes evident. It is surely no accident that they work in the shadow of two sta-tues not often found in country graveyards. We first see them enter from behind a statue of Death and then take their places in a tableau of the Crucifixion. The scene is lit by the evening sky, the three crosses are carefully askew, and the echo unmistakable. They put their clothes on a stick; Frankenstein pulls out a stake from the grave and casually plants it to form another cross. As they haul up the casket in front of a statue of Christ crucified, the empty black clothes between the cross and the figure of Death form another, omi-nous Calvary. That Whale built the scene is made clear by the hat on the stake, which neither character is wearing when he enters. Frankenstein's line as he holds the casket is signifi-cant: "He is just resting, waiting for a new life to come." The scene is a perverse Resurrection, and the Monster des-tined to parody Christ.

The next scene carries forth both images as Frankenstein and Fritz climb a jagged studio mountain to cut down a hanged man for their collection of raw materials. Fritz scales the gibbet while Frankenstein holds a lantern, which is given some prominence. Like the figure of Death brooding over the graveyard, the lantern is prophetic. Fire comes to represent the power Frankenstein will hold in his hands and the destruction it will cause. Fritz carries the lantern down the steps of the tower when he lets in Waldman, Victor Moritz, and Elizabeth, while the sparking equipment illuminates the creation scene they witness. For a moment, Frankenstein controls the explosive power of the lightning bolt and uses it to give the Monster life; everyone else cringes in fear for his own life.

The "education" of the Monster is also presented through images of light. When it lifts its hands to the skylight, only to see it shut, we realize that one possibility has been closed off forever. Heavenly light is replaced by hellfire; a burning torch is used to scourge the Monster and goad it to violence. The contrast is pointed up in one marvelous scene. Fritz jabs the torch at the Monster, shouting "Ha! Here's fire for you!" in a weirdly off-center stone dungeon. In the background, through a small barred window, rays of sunlight struggle through. Sunlight will bathe the creature for only one moment — when it almost finds happiness floating flowers with the little girl.

The conclusion of the film returns to the actual and symbolic locale of its opening. The villagers, armed with torches, split up into two groups. Frankenstein leads one contingent through the barren countryside. Before his "conversion" Frankenstein gave a misshapen being unnatural life; now he drives a mob to destroy what it cannot accept. Cut off from his followers, he confronts the Monster on the same spot where the gibbet of the hanged murderer once stood. Whale cuts back and forth between them, uniting them. The action stops for a moment, and we realize that the Monster has come to a new level of awareness. It strides to its maker and brushes aside his torch. Losing his symbol of power and control, Frankenstein suddenly screams for help. For a brief moment, the Monster is in command and carries its maker off to an old windmill. The structure reminds us of the tower and, in fact, one draft of the script set the laboratory in the mill. In any case, the meaning is clear; scientist and Monster are tied together in creation and destruction. The trip to the old mill is a cinematic equivalent of the long journey in Mary Shelley's novel from Geneva to the frozen expanse near the Arctic Circle. On that journey, Frankenstein was aware that he and the Monster were doubles; the same realization touches Whale's *Frankenstein*. Karloff and Clive face each other through the revolving mill wheel; a flickering shot alternating between both faces dramatically makes them one — they wear exactly the same expression.

After the Monster throws Frankenstein to the mob, they call for its death and use their torches to set fire to the mill. It is a fitting conclusion to both motifs. As Frankenstein falls, he hangs for a moment on the blades of the windmill. These same blades form, in the final fadeout, a gigantic cross on top of a bleak hill. The Monster, trapped under the weight of a great beam, is finally returned to Calvary. The mob, given the thief who stole life from God, destroys the being forsaken by its creator.

The movie should have ended here. Only a few days before the film was finished, and after the initial previews, a Hollywood epilogue was added. We see Frankenstein recuperating, while the Baron and maids toast the future. The ending is so obviously tacked on that it fails to destroy the impact of the double death at the windmill. Whale's Christian imagery there, and throughout the film, was meant to be seen ironically — the same impulse dubbed eighteenth-century graverobbers "resurrectionists." However, in equating the Monster with Christ and not Satan, Whale made clear his differences with Mrs. Shelley. In a sense, he kills off the Monster when, in the novel, it still is "innocent" — before it vows destruction on all that Frankenstein loves. At that point, the guilt clearly rests on the Monster's creator and an unfeeling world. The image of the burning cross, which must have had strong associations in the thirties when the Klan was at its height, points up the mob mindlessness that does the Monster in. The final fire is only an extension of the torch wielded by Fritz to torment what he feared and therefore hated. Mordaunt Hall, reviewing *Frankenstein* in the December 5, 1931, issue of the *New York Times* recognized the "disturbing nature" of this "artistically conceived work" when he described the soundtrack of the Monster's death: "From the screen comes the sound of the crackling of the blazing woodwork, the hue and cry of the frightened populace, and the queer sounds of the dying monster."

The phenomenal commercial success of *Frankenstein* inspired, four years later, its first and best sequel. James Whale's *The Bride of Frankenstein* again starred Colin Clive, Karloff (temporarily shorn of his first name), Valerie Hobson as a new Elizabeth, and Elsa Lanchester in a dual role as "The Mate" and Mary Shelley herself. The film opens with an "historical" prologue. Bryon, Shelley, Mary, and four huge Russian wolfhounds gather around a baronial fireplace while an electrical storm rages outside; all but the dogs discuss the implications of her story of "the punishments that befell a mortal man who dared to emulate God." That the story they refer to is the 1931 screenplay, and not the novel, becomes evident when Mary Shelley reveals to the breathless pair that "the Monster didn't die in the fire at the burning mill." This clumsy attempt at authenticity, while cinematically unnecessary, provides a clue to the impulse behind *The*

Bride of Frankenstein. The film takes up Whale's interpretation of Mary Shelley's story with no lapse of time, beginning exactly where and when the last film left off. The two can almost be seen as one. Although *The Bride of Frankenstein* is a more elaborate, more bizarre, more darkly comic production, it continues retelling the myth after the Monster has lost its innocence and science has gained knowledge of the secrets of life.

Whale's desire to tie the two films together as closely as possible extended even to Karloff's make-up, which was altered to account for the Monster's (offscreen) fall from the burning mill into a watery cistern underneath. Most of its hair is singed away, part of its face is burned, and its one black suit is torn and stained. More importantly, its ignorance and innocence are gone. Whale points this up through the ironies of the opening sequence. The parents of little Maria, whom the Monster accidentally drowned in the first film, wait by the wreckage of the still smouldering mill to be sure the Monster is dead. The father enters the ruin to investigate, falls through the floor, and is promptly strangled and drowned by the Monster, who climbs out and does the same to his wife. As it rises from the pool of water (a nice Freudian touch) we realize that this second resurrection will be even more deadly than the first. Full of hatred, the Monster wanders off into the world.

Soon after, back at the castle, Frankenstein's anguished recovery is interrupted by a booming knock at the door. When his comic servant, Minnie (a new character), answers with a great bustling and the words, "All right, don't knock the castle over, we're not all dead yet!" the tone of the film is set. The door opens, and in stalks the maddest of all mad scientists, the notorious Dr. Pretorious (played with manic effectiveness by skeletal Ernest Thesiger). His name is significant (obviously so, since Minnie hollers out "Pretorious" at least five times). It combines the Latin for "causing to be known" and "of the ruling class"; like Frankenstein, he is obsessed with creating life, but not to aid mankind or even solely to glorify himself. He wishes simply to rule the rest of humanity, whom he regards with contempt as inferiors. His handiwork, which he takes out of a casket-shaped case to show Frankenstein, consists of a grotesque collection of homunculi sealed in glass jars and dressed as mermaid, devil, ballerina, bishop, king, and queen. Pretorious' black costume, his medieval skullcap, and the archaic wax-sealed ribbons on his jars clearly make him a "new alchemist," who needs the technological know-how of Frankenstein to turn his own small madness into a method for ruling the world. Pretorious has a glass of gin ("It's my only weakness") with Franken- stein, and proposes a toast "To a new world of gods and mon- sters!" Gone is the desire to create a perfect being — the goal now is a perfect weapon. The character of Pretorious surely owes something to the rise of Hitler in the four years since the 1931 film. The altruistic (if insane) Frankenstein is to be used by the fascistic and somewhat perverse Pretorious. Hitler's "New Order" and Pretorious' "New World" spell the same disaster for the human race.

Humanity doesn't come off much better in this film than the scientists. While Pretorious is plotting the future, the Monster saves a drowning shepherdess, only to be shot by misunderstanding hunters. The scene comes straight from the novel; in both *Frankenstein*s it occurs soon after, as Mary Shelley's Monster puts it, "the mildness of my nature had fled, and all within me was turned to gall and bitterness." In novel and film the act seems somewhat out of char- acter. Mrs. Shelley probably added the episode as a Romantic set piece — "rustics" and shepherdesses were a part of nearly every literary landscape. In the film, it may suggest that, although the Monster is no longer innocent, it is still capable of acts of kindness and able to be redeemed by human love. This interpretation is strengthened by the next scene, which faintly recalls the De Lacey episode but gives it a different twist. The Monster wanders into an isolated hut, where a blind hermit gives it refuge. In an episode that straddles the thin line between the pathetic and the ludicrous, the Monster finds a friend. It learns to talk, drink, and smoke; puffing on an after dinner cigar, it listens to the hermit play "Ave Maria" on his violin. The irony is that the Monster can only find its brief happiness with another outcast, and a blind one at that. As soon as another hunter shows up to ask directions, the Monster is doomed. In fact, they are both doomed. In the confusion of discovery, a fire burns down the cottage, the hermit is led off, and the Monster escapes, calling for its only friend.

Whale's use of misty "romantic" close-ups and a syrupy soundtrack is more evidence for his ironic viewpoint and another cinematic joke — the love scene at its least lovely. But it also points up the absurdity of the Monster ever living a domestic existence, while introducing another spate of Whale's weird Christian symbolism. The hermit wears a monk's robe; his choice of music and sustenance — he feeds the Monster bread and wine — make this the Monster's last and only supper. After this brief communion, it escapes to a surrealistic forest of bare tree trunks and is captured by a mob of villagers. They truss it to a stake and hoist it in the air; for one short moment it hangs suspended, a grotesque Christ, before it falls into a hay wagon and is hauled into the village. There, the mob chains it to a great throne in a dungeon and torments it some more. It easily escapes, pulling off its chains and ripping off the cell door. The scene owes more to *King Kong* (1933) than to the Gospel, but the effect is the same — our sympathy goes to the prisoner, who has superhuman power and a strange nobility. Pursued by the howling mob once again, the Monster heads for a graveyard where, in sight of the same figure of Death that brooded over the opening sequences of Whale's first *Frankenstein*, it overturns the statue of a bishop and invades the tomb. The overall religious imagery is more playful here than in the last film, but it does accentuate the uniqueness of the Monster and returns the mythic relationships of *Frankenstein* to their most perplexing level. Man may be guilty of rejecting Christ, but what responsibility does it have for the Monster? If Frankenstein and Pretorious are would-be gods, then the Monster is their forsaken and misshapen Son. But it is a reverse Christ; rather than Harrowing Hell, the Monster finds a home in the world of the dead.

In the crypt it runs into Pretorious, who is enjoying a slabside picnic after a bit of graverobbing. The two necrophiles strike up a friendship, especially after he promises to build a mate for the Monster. Pretorious and the Monster become the prime movers in the final creation scene; in a sequence probably inspired in part by gangster films, Pretorious and his inhuman henchman strong-arm Frankenstein into helping out by kidnapping his own bride and hiding her in a cave. Her life depends upon Frankenstein's giving life to the Monster's bride. Reluctantly, he sets to work, back in the tower, spurred on by Pretorious' frenetic enthusiasm and the Monster's timely growls. The Mate's brain has been grown artificially by Pretorious (no formaldehyde-soaked criminal brain this time around) so that it will truly be a blank slate. Its heart has been supplied by Dwight Frye, playing another assistant, with a new name, Karl, and a hump reduced to a limp. In the original script, he was sent to get a heart at the morgue but extracted Elizabeth's instead. In the mellower final version, he kills a villager to get it, then comments too rashly to Frankenstein, "It's a very fresh one!" Finally, wrapped in bandages, and of a considerably better lineage than the Karloff Monster, the bride-to-be awaits the spark of life.

The creation scene is more extravagant than ever. The tower has had some renovations; it is taller, with more elaborate (and appropriately phallic) equipment, while lightning is attracted by giant kites Karl releases from the roof. Whale's techniques are similarly less restrained. He cuts madly from dials to hands to a heart, to sparking equipment, to optically prolonged shots of lightning, keeping up a mad staccato rhythm, building to an inevitable climax. In his first *Frankenstein,* a surreal mood was suggested by the angled expressionist sets; here, the camera itself is often tilted sharply — a device copied later in the "Batman" television series to serve much the same satirical purpose.[5] At the moment of birth, Karl falls to his death — a life for a life — and the slab is lowered from the roof. For the second time (and the second Monster) Frankenstein shouts, "She's alive! ALIVE!" The table is tilted up (this piece of equipment becomes a stock cinematic laboratory prop) and the Mate's eyes open, while her hands jerk forward.

In the next shot, the bandages are gone from her face. We see the effeminate Pretorious and Frankenstein standing on either side, the symbolic parents of the Mate. They have dressed her in a white wedding "shroud." A series of close-ups of the face reveals a Nefertiti hairdo streaked by a lightning bolt of silver hair, lips smeared with color, and skin mapped with scars. It is, all in all, a much neater job than the first Monster. In a final bit of impish humor, the soundtrack fills with church bells as Pretorious shouts, "The Bride of Frankenstein!" Despite the four-star wedding, the marriage is short-lived. Although her body is a corpse, the bride's brain has never been dead; her natural reaction to the Monster is disgust and horror. She recoils from its clumsy advances with a resounding hiss. Announcing "We belong dead!" the Monster finds the convenient destruct lever and blows the tower to atoms. Pretorious' new world of gods and monsters dies at the altar.

Of course, this scene is first and foremost crackling good cinema, the resounding catastrophe we all relish. But it is also an attempt to update Mary Shelley's message to examine the new science, its monsters, and mankind. The novel's Victor Frankenstein, in a passage that inspired the conclusion of the film, wondered about the implications of creating a mate for the Monster: "They might even hate each other . . . She might also turn with disgust from him . . . Even if they were to leave Europe . . . one of the first results of those sympathies for which the daemon thirsted would be children, and a race of devils would be propagated upon the earth, who might make the very existence of the species of man a condition precarious and full of terror." It is obvious that the "science" of creating life in both Frankenstein films is not taken seriously. The early nineteenth-century belief in the imminent discovery of the secret of life had, by the nineteen thirties, become quite dated. But the possibility of a "race of devils" and the science to create them were contemporary fears.

Early in the film, we learn that Pretorious' own technique was to grow people "as nature does, from seed." At one point, he prevents his miniature King Henry VIII from getting at his tiny ballerina. He is, then, more interested in controlling the natural breeding of his creatures to obtain his "gods and monsters" than in building them out of corpses. He enlists Frankenstein's help only to obtain the female he needs to continue his own genetic experiments on a grander scale. The mad dream he carries around in his little jars and hopes to impose upon the world was a current one; the science is eugenics. Contemporary Nazi mythology promised a race of men like gods, created through selective breeding and elimination of the defective and inferior. Through Pretorious, Whale shows us the true nature of that dream — the gods are indistinguishable from the monsters.

Pretorious is a perfect parody of a would-be Hitler. His passion to breed a new race compensates for his own apparent homosexuality and perverse love of death. He keeps his jars in a casket and eats lunch on a tombstone. Whale makes clear that if Pretorious ever were to succeed, he would make the world a cemetery. Frankenstein turns out to be little better. He first cooperates with Pretorious reluctantly, in order to save Elizabeth, but soon gets swept up in the glory of his achievement. At the second creation, he is as triumphant as Pretorious, and equally responsible. It is up to the monsters, the manipulated victims, to assert the proper priorities. The Mate rejects the future selected for it, and the Monster recognizes that there can be no place in the land of the living for creatures of death. It tells Elizabeth and Frankenstein to go and includes Pretorious among those who "belong dead."

The survival of Frankenstein recalls the escape of Walton in the novel while suggesting, as the presence of Dr. Waldman did in the first film, that there is a "good" science needed to combat the black arts of the new alchemy. But this conclusion was only stitched in at the last moment. If you look closely at the final holocaust, Frankenstein is present. In the shooting script he was slated to perish along with the rest. When it was decided at the last moment to spare him (for the second time), probably as a concession to the standard Hollywood ending, the laboratory explosion had already been filmed. It was hoped, rightly, that the audience's attention would focus on the exploding equipment and ignore the extra victim.

The black comedy of *The Bride of Frankenstein* only darkens the bleak vision of the earlier film. Men are either hunters or a tormenting mob; their future is determined by a group of bizarre misfits playing God in a lonely tower, acting out fantasies of power and destruction. The Monster must decide where they all belong and become, finally, the unlikely savior of humanity. The blend of fascist lunacy, religious allegory, and gallows humor that is *The Bride of Frankenstein* has a feeling about it of helplessness before a future that was becoming clearer and more terrifying all the time. Mussolini, already in power for many years, was about to invade Ethiopia; Hitler, whose New Order was two years old in 1935, was giving life to a huge disciplined war machine and preaching the myth of Aryan superiority. The cataclysmic ending of Whale's last *Frankenstein* film is, like the ending of the novel, safely remote from the rest of humanity, but the tone of the film and the ambiguity of its conclusion hold out little hope for a future free of madmen or monsters.

CHAPTER VII

Frankenstein Descending

Mr. Karloff's best make-up should not be permitted to pass from the screen. The Monster should become an institution, like Charlie Chan ...

New York Times REVIEW OF
The Bride of Frankenstein
May 11, 1935

THE *New York Times* REVIEWER, Frank S. Nugent, needn't have worried. The Karloff Monster (with and without Boris himself) developed a catlike ability to escape even the most obliterating catastrophes more or less intact. In the ten years after *The Bride of Frankenstein* it returned in *Son of Frankenstein, The Ghost of Frankenstein, Frankenstein Meets the Wolf Man, House of Frankenstein* and *House of Dracula* played, in order, by Karloff, Lon Chaney, Jr., Bela Lugosi, Glenn Strange, and Glenn Strange again, with occasional stand-ins by stuntmen Bud Wolfe and Edwin Parker. Aside from minor changes to accommodate the different physiognomies of the actors under the gashes and greasepaint, the Monster returned to the contours and muteness of Whale's first film. In fact, Whale's two films each inspired its own branch of the Frankenstein tradition. Part One, with its silent Monster and well-meaning but misdirected scientist, became the basis of Universal Studio's many sequels, which in turn firmly established a pattern that would influence science fiction and horror films through the fifties and sixties. *The Bride of Frankenstein*, with its articulate Monster and cold, perverse "Pretorian" scientist, was, for the time being, forgotten. Late in the fifties these characters returned to inspire a whole new Frankenstein cycle. But first, the concerns of the forties prevailed, and Frankenstein, symbolically at least, joined a world at war.

The forties cycle of horror movies was, of course, not confined to *Frankenstein* remakes. The Hollywood monster factories were going at full scream. Old thirties creatures like the Mummy, the Invisible Man, and Dracula returned; the Wolf Man, Invisible Woman, Leopard Man, Ape Woman, Cat People, and assorted zombies and gorillas joined the war effort, while Dracula enlisted a son. At Universal, monsters made guest appearances on each other's turf, dragging along perennial favorites like gypsy woman Maria Ouspenskaya and hunchback-turned-villager Dwight Frye.[1] As discussed earlier, the reasons for the appeal of horror lie deep in the realm of nightmare. Like bad dreams themselves, the films project images that portray the monstrous impulses within each of us. Walter Evans argues quite cleverly that the wolf men whose palms turn hairy by the light of the full moon, the monsters with ungainly bodies and misdirected libidos, and the scientists who abandon their fiancées to create life in secret laboratories, are related to adolescent anxieties about sex.[2] But the timing of the cycle suggests that the traditional appeal was given a new impetus — the real horrors of the Second World War.

Some horror films dealt directly with the conflict. In *The Return of the Vampire* (1944), Dracula is revived in the blitz and terrorizes London. The Invisible Man was recruited in 1942 and became *The Invisible Agent*. More often though, the Europe of horror films has no Nazis and, indeed, no direct references to the war at all. Of course, fantastic films exist in the nonspecific world of the imagination; too close a fidelity to outside realities would spoil the suspension of disbelief that keeps the monsters alive. But within the horror conventions, political fears took hold. In the Universal films, werewolves, vampires, hunchbacks, and mad scientists wander the back roads of the Old World, refugees looking for an elusive cure, or more often, an opportunity to stir up more mayhem. It is taken for granted by moviegoer and monster alike that the destruction of each creature can only be temporary — there is no final resolution. Even films set in America, like *Son of Dracula* (1943), deal with the "infection" of a new land by old, European diseases. The war years meant an indefinite suspension of the happy ending that, in Hollywood, resolves the conflicts of youth. Those waiting at home were aware that when the "boys" returned, they would be boys no longer. All of these feelings could be, and were, incorporated into the horror film. For the lineage of Frankenstein, war meant the power of technology wedded to fascism, translated into an undying Monster used for destructive purposes by a new and dangerous master.

Son of Frankenstein (1939) sported a big budget, a good cast that included Basil Rathbone, Boris Karloff, Bela Lugosi, and Lionel Atwill, stylish sets, and a literate script by Willis Cooper; yet, marred by director Rowland Lee's slow pacing and Rathbone's histrionics, it pales by comparison to its predecessors. The best moments are provided by Lugosi's excellent characterization of Ygor, the Monster's demented keeper. The deformities of Fritz and Karl are recalled by Ygor's broken neck, the result of an unsuccessful execution for grave robbing. Ygor (the name has become almost a generic term for deformed assistants) has varied abilities; he not only plays eerie recorder tunes in the ruins of the old laboratory, but sews his monstrous friend a new sheepskin vest to replace, for this film at least, its basic black suit. Despite his domesticity, Ygor is a much more menacing figure than either of his two cinematic ancestors, since he has absolute control of the Monster and murderous plans.

Karloff, as the Monster, has little to do in much of the film but lie unconscious on a slab. The first convention is established; the Monster "cannot die" but is perpetually sick and will need the help of an unending series of doctors to make it well again. The first of these is Wolf Frankenstein (Basil Rathbone in his pre–Sherlock Holmes days), who has returned to the homestead twenty-five years after his father's death. Ygor brings him to the Monster and asks him to cure his "friend"; after some initial hesitation, Wolf sets up the old lab equipment and gives the Monster a revivifying jolt. Though at first it doesn't seem to work, the Monster soon takes to walking the halls of the castle and visiting Wolf's young son, Peter, who enjoys playing with the "giant." We learn of this scene secondhand. Only slightly more emphasis is given to the fact that Ygor has been using the Monster as a kind of "smart bomb," sending it out to kill the members of the jury who sent him to the gallows. The deficiencies of *Son of Frankenstein* as a film are suggested by these two missed opportunities. Karloff is only given a few moments to let the Monster show a glimmer of its former "humanity." Its howling response to Ygor's death and kindness toward Peter do little to offset the general impression that the Monster is no more than a weapon. In a raucous climax, it engages Police Inspector Krogh and Wolf in a wild battle that ends when Frankenstein manages, Tarzan style, to knock it over a ledge into a convenient pool of molten sulfur. Victim to the end, the Monster is revived only to be used and abused, sent out to kill and then be destroyed.

Whether or not the prewar atmosphere had something to do with altering the image of the Monster from isolated outcast to controlled weapon, and transforming its caretaker and "friend" from scientist to criminal, it certainly contributed a new member to the Frankenstein troupe. The bumbling Baron and burgomeister of the earlier movies are replaced in *Son of Frankenstein* by the crisply authoritarian Krogh, played by Lionel Atwill. Except for a mad doctor stint in *The Ghost of Frankenstein* (1942), Atwill plays an identical role in all of the films of this series, always dressed in a shiny comic opera costume which looks like a Hollywood parody of German officialdom. As Krogh, he has both a monocle and a wooden arm to hold it, his own arm having been torn off in childhood by the Monster. When he swivels his arm up with an audible screech, viewers in 1939 couldn't help but be reminded of the hordes of German soldiers and civilians giving the mindless, stiff-armed Nazi salute. At the end of *Son of Frankenstein*, the Monster rips off the wooden arm and swings it around its head, in a momentary triumph of victim against authority and a nice bit of macabre film making.

Wolf Frankenstein is the first of the "mad" doctors who largely replace mad scientists like Pretorious and Henry Frankenstein. Like his brother Ludwig in *The Ghost of Frankenstein*, Dr. Mannering in *Frankenstein Meets the Wolf Man*, and Dr. Edelmann in *House of Dracula*, Wolf is a medical man, who first examines the Monster reluctantly, and then is obsessed with the idea of seeing it "restored to full strength." None of them are researchers after the secrets of life and death, and two are psychiatrists. Most of their Monster-making knowledge comes from the "old Frankenstein records," which Colin Clive entrusted to Dr. Waldman in the 1931 film. Like the Monster itself, they have a way of showing up with astonishing ease. In purely political terms, the change from scientist to doctor is logical; the "Monster" contemplated in earlier films is here and seems immortal — it is up to the doctors of body and mind to repair a world that has grown monstrous and gone mad. In at least two films, they have to contend with the brain of Ygor, who wants the Monster for his criminal schemes of death and power; his simple-minded viciousness replaces the refinements of Pretorious and is more suited to the straightforward savagery of war. All of the doctors set out to destroy or cure the Monster, but, by allowing their egotism to awaken the sleeping giant, only give Ygor a tool for magnifying his own destructiveness. Their ineffectual attempts to fix things, and the ease with which Ygor uses them, underline the danger that is loose in the world. Each film, from *Son of Frankenstein* on, ends in momentary victory for mankind, with the almost certain assurance that the Monster will rise again.

The Ghost of Frankenstein resurrects both Lugosi as Ygor and the Monster, played this time in stodgy fashion by Lon Chaney, Jr.; Lionel Atwill is back, accompanied by Sir Cedric Hardwicke as Ludwig Frankenstein, Doctor of the Mind, and an hilariously miscast Ralph Bellamy dashing about in a white suit and riding boots as public prosecutor Eric Ernst. Dwight Frye even appears for a moment leading the inevitable mob of villagers, but the spirit of the original *Frankenstein* is indeed only a ghost. The one memorable scene is with a little girl the Monster befriends. In all of the Frankenstein films, and as far back as Wegener's 1920 film *The Golem*, the Monster had been linked to children, the only people who don't run from it in horror. Their reaction contrasts sharply with that of William Frankenstein in the novel; he responds with an instinctive loathing that emphasizes the unnaturalness of Mary Shelley's Monster. The movie Monster is seen almost as another child, an orphan raised to do evil by wicked, uncaring adults. In *The Ghost of Frankenstein*, the Monster helps the girl retrieve her toy, a large ball on a string. Of course, the townspeople believe it will hurt her, so they coax it down and attack it, causing it to kill one of them. After a bit more adult duplicity, they manage to capture it for a while. Later, the Monster kidnaps the girl and goes back to get the ball. As the lumbering Monster carries her off, dragging the ball by the string, we glimpse the spark of innocence still smoldering inside the much-tortured human junk heap the Monster has become.

The Ghost of Frankenstein introduces one of the most popular operations in horror movies to the *Frankenstein* saga —

the brain transplant. Everyone has a candidate for the Monster's new brain, depending upon his own hopes for the future. Ludwig, wanting to correct the mistakes of his illustrious ancestor, chooses kindly Dr. Kettering, murdered by the Monster. The Monster itself chooses innocence, kidnapping the little girl in order to borrow her brain. Atwill, as the evil Dr. Bohmer, manages to slip Ygor's brain into the body of the Monster, after he is promised a place in Ygor's projected dictatorship. Ygor's literally twisted mind has hatched a political plot. The Monster will be a one-man army, giving him "the strength of a hundred men" and the means to "rule the country." The joining of deformity and brute power brings together the elements of the myth that reflect the political realities of 1942. The Monster awakens from the operation and announces, "I, Ygor, will live forever!" Frankenstein cries, "The crime of my father is now mine, but a thousandfold!" Fortunately, Ygor's blood and the Monster's don't mix; instead of eternal life, or even a rule that will last a thousand years, all Ygor gets is blindness and a losing bout with the inevitable conflagration.

Frankenstein Meets the Wolf Man (1943) is best passed over quickly. Aside from a nicely chilling opening sequence in a cemetery, the movie is notable for Bela Lugosi's execrable stint as the Monster and the incomprehensible gaps in the plot. Both were partly the fault of a last-minute editing job. Originally, the Monster was to be blind and speak with Ygor's voice, continuing from *The Ghost of Frankenstein.* In the final release print, all scenes with the Monster talking and any references to its blindness were cut. As a result, the Monster's stiff-armed groping is never explained, though ironically it contributed to the transition of the Monster's public image from a feeling being to a mindless robot. The plot is simple and predictable. Dr. Mannering, like Ludwig Frankenstein, starts his operation intending to kill the Monster but decides

Frankenstein *Descending*

he has to "see it at its full power." The seduction of power backfires; Wolf Man and Monster clash in a violent battle until the villagers (among them Dwight Frye) explode a convenient dam, washing them both to the next film. The "battle of the monsters" is clearly the only reason for the movie; although it fits the mood of wartime, *Frankenstein Meets the Wolf Man* is really a mindless exercise, reducing the subtleties of the tradition to little more than the Monster's blind violence.

Mindlessness is certainly a theme in *House of Frankenstein* (1944); in this case it is interpreted quite literally in an obsession with brain transplants. After leaving the *Frankenstein* series at Universal, Boris Karloff went over to Columbia, where he made a series of quickie "mad doctor" films. His experiments all backfired, though the movies didn't — they managed to make respectable amounts of money. As a result, Karloff came back in *House of Frankenstein* as Dr. Gustav Niemann, the only certified mad doctor in the series, having been locked in an insane asylum for trying to transplant a man's brain into a dog. After escaping with Daniel, his hunchback (of course) assistant, he manages to revive Dracula and thaw out the Wolf Man and Frankenstein Monster, who have been neatly frozen in the ruins of the dam. Like Ygor in *Son of Frankenstein*, he uses the monsters to revenge himself on those who had him imprisoned. This generally awful movie has a few unintentionally funny moments. The best is when Niemann plans a marathon brain switch involving the Monster, the Wolf Man, and two of his enemies. When Daniel is left odd brain out, he begins the general catastrophe that ends the picture. The Monster is barely given time to rise from the operating table and grunt (it's sick again) before it is driven into quicksand with Niemann. *House of Frankenstein* is really a Gothic vaudeville show, where each monster gets to do its act, then is disposed of just in time for the next one to growl center stage. Even the subplot, between Daniel and a gypsy girl, is clearly taken from the Quasimodo-Esmeralda relationship of the latest Charles Laughton version of *The Hunchback of Notre Dame* (1939). Originality was flagging, along with audience interest — the Universal *Frankenstein* series was obviously dying out.

Yet before Abbott and Costello met Frankenstein in 1948 and delivered the coup de grâce, one more film intervened. Erle Kenton's *House of Dracula* (1945) contained many of the familiar elements, including all three monsters and a Jekyll/Hyde Dr. Edelmann, modeled on the Spencer Tracy portrayal four years previously. Despite the staleness of the formula, this film is in many ways delightful, marked by touches of offbeat humor and parody as well as some optimistic twists that show a fond familiarity with the traditional elements of the genre. Dr. Edelmann's assistant, for example, is first shown in a soft focus close-up. She is a beautiful woman and, we expect, destined to be the standard vapid heroine. Slowly the camera moves back and we discover that she is a whiteclad hunchback who turns out not to be a demented dwarf, but the moral force in the film. Edelmann is, at least at first, a kind and quite sane psychiatrist, who sets out to cure both Dracula and the Wolf Man. In an early scene, while the Wolf Man waits in the outer office, Edelmann gives Dracula one of his "treatments," commenting, "Your next appointment will be Thursday evening, same time." A bit later, he reassures Lawrence (Wolf Man) Talbot (played by Lon Chaney, Jr.), who has locked himself up in Lionel Atwill's jail cell, that "there is no such thing as a werewolf, it's all in your mind!" Unfortunately, Talbot begins to sprout hair at that moment, forcing Edelmann to change his diagnosis to a combination of "pressure on the brain" and "abnormal hormones." All of this absurdity is pointed up by a weird character (played by Skelton Knaggs), who appears periodically to whisper lines like, "Strange business, if you ask me."

It's possible to see the obsession with brain transplants in the earlier films as influenced, in part, by a contemporary fear of psychoanalysts, who seemed to many to have mysterious, almost supernatural power, suggested by the popular title of "head shrinker." At the same time, it was another manifestation of wartime concerns. Fear of a fifth column and the power of propaganda showed up in many war films; even the zombie movies made at the time gained their horror from the idea that human beings could be made into mindless slaves. In the Frankenstein films, the brain transplant symbolized the power of science to change and control the personality. Edelmann is refreshingly different. He uses his ability at instant diagnosis and a secret "skull-softening" technique literally to expand the Wolf Man's head, relieving the "pressure on the brain" and curing Lon Chaney Jr., of his horrid hirsuteness.

After Edelmann finds the Monster conveniently washed into a cave near his hospital, he falls into the now familiar pattern of renovating his laboratory and attempting to revive it. Edelmann's motives are, however, purely humanitarian. He must try to cure the Monster because of his responsibility to aid the sick, whether they be men or monsters. The expected disaster is literally short-circuited after the following somewhat stilted conversation with Nina, his assistant:

Edelmann: Can man sit in judgment over life and death?
Nina: What man creates he can also destroy.
Edelmann: That would be murder! My responsibility is to this helpless body.
Nina: Man's responsibility is to his fellow man.
Edelmann: Perhaps you're right, Nina. Frankenstein's Monster must never wreak havoc again.

He turns off the equipment, scoring a victory for humanity and restoring the good name of doctors everywhere. This outcome, which may owe something to the optimism that accompanied the end of the war, is unfortunately short-lived. Edelmann is infected with vampire blood and goes quite mad. He returns to his laboratory and, in some great atmospheric shots projecting his enormous shadow against a giant door, stalks around preparing to learn "the secret of immortality" by animating the Monster. In a last bit of humor, just as the machinery reaches a crescendo, it blows a tube and goes dead. Edelmann finally manages to revive the Monster for about ten seconds. It blunders into its third fire (second actually — the footage was scissored out of *The Ghost of Frankenstein*) and falls to a final confrontation with Abbott and Costello. This film, aptly named *Abbott and Costello Meet Frankenstein*, has been variously described as a travesty on the classic films and a faithful piece of satire. It is, in either case, pretty thin stuff, marked by the contrast between the idiocies of Lou Costello and the pathetic earnestness of Lon Chaney, Jr., and Bela Lugosi taking their famous Monsters out for a last airing. As a faithful, witty, and coherent conclusion to the Universal series, *House of Dracula* stands up much better.

The legacy of the post–Whale Frankenstein cycle included an emphasis upon the Monster as an eternal nuisance and potential weapon, and the scientist (with one exception) as a well-meaning character who allows his own vanity and scientific curiosity to get the better of him. It is up to the inevitable band of villagers to burn the house, blow up the dam, chase the Monster into a swamp, or otherwise take their destiny into their own hands. The ambiguity of the Whale films and the complexity of Karloff's creature are largely gone, while Mrs. Shelley's novel is almost totally forgotten. The ritual energizing of the dormant creature and its casting out by the villagers do, however, dimly reflect the opposition of science and society that Mrs. Shelley found inherent in Frankenstein's experiments. In the fifties, though the Universal Monster seemed finally consigned to oblivion, this same pattern returned, on a grander scale, to give form to the greater dangers of the post-Hiroshima age.

From the flying saucer scare that started in the late forties came *The Thing* (1951), directed by Christian Nyby reportedly with the help of Howard Hawks. The isolated village of the Frankenstein series is here transferred to an Air Force station in the Arctic, but the same figures return. After the discovery of an alien vegetable man frozen in the familiar block of ice, we only need wait a few minutes for the expected thaw. Again, we have a well-meaning scientist who tries to understand the creature and even takes to growing its seeds and nourishing them on human blood. But, as in the post-Whale Frankenstein cycle, the film is solidly on the side of the "villagers." They destroy the multiplying alien seedlings just in time, then "cook" the vegetable man with the scientific torch of electricity. When we finally glimpse the alien, we are not surprised that it looks like a bald Frankenstein Monster.

The Thing is a transition piece; two years later, atomic experiments in the Arctic released *The Beast from 20,000 Fathoms*, featuring the first of a host of gigantic creatures which, as the Japanese can best attest, continually emerged to test man's defenses. In each of these films, a creature comes from the waste places of the world — either the desert, the ocean floor, or the Arctic (where, of course, Mary Shelley's Monster disappeared) — to threaten all of mankind. It is often awakened from a long hibernation by atomic tests or some other ill-conceived experiment; after a few isolated attacks on outlying human settlements, it heads for the centers of civilization. Penetrating the elaborate defenses of the military, it enters the heart of a major city (New York, Tokyo, and Washington are prime targets) and proceeds to tear it apart. The Monster is finally destroyed by some last-ditch stratagem or exotic scientific device, but everyone concerned knows that mankind has only been reprieved. The films invariably end with a warning; either, as in *The Thing*, they tell us to "Keep watching the skies!" or, more commonly, they repeat a variation of the ritual phrase "There are things man is not meant to know." It is taken for granted that science will revive more monsters, and mankind will need to keep casting them out.

The giant creatures of the fifties are not of the same species as the Frankenstein Monster, though they have much the same function and share a common ancestor. On the cultural level, monsters visualize and exorcise group anxieties. The forties monsters were linked to the relatively tame horrors of World War II; with the growth of our technology and its potential for destruction, the monsters grew in size and destructiveness. The popularity of giant monsters in the midfifties in America, and from then until now in Japan, visualize and exorcise our fear of the atomic bomb and Japan's experience with it. The bomb shelter craze and the Monster craze complemented each other; one madly prepared for an indescribable fear, the other attempted to confront that fear in some tangible form.[3] At the same time, the popularity of all monsters owes something to what Freud called the "inclination to aggression ... the cause of hostility against which all civilizations have to struggle." [4] Like the monsters of myth, these creatures, whether reptilian or near human, are a modern expression of the spontaneous, natural, irrational and primitive emotions that delight in destruction.[5] The Frankenstein Monster is often equated with a child because its hatred for the adult world that casts it out is childlike in its rage and simplicity. The giant dinosaurs, insects, and crustaceans are all relics of a past age, literally primitive remnants of the childhood of earth, returned to battle with a grown-up world. The conflict that ensues in all these films is the struggle between order and disorder, suppression and aggression, that is as old as society itself.

Consequently, in the decade following 1948, Mary Shelley's Monster lay dormant, making its presence felt indirectly. In order to find direct connections with the myth, it is necessary to look in a most unlikely place. Makers of "serious" science fiction films often try to dissociate themselves from mad scientists and monsters; yet the myth still influences them. It shows up through the sixties, in films like *Dr. Strangelove* (1964), *2001: A Space Odyssey* (1968), or *Colossus: The Forbin Project* (1970), where the survival of humanity is threatened by a conflict between "mad" or at least misdirected science and machinery designed to be near perfect and almost human, which turns rebellious and monstrous. In 1956 one of the most elaborate science fiction films ever made, *Forbidden Planet*, used dazzling special effects to project us across time and space, examining the future of technology in terms familiar to anyone who has gone no further than Mrs. Shelley's novel, or a Frankenstein movie.

Forbidden Planet is set in the year 2200 A.D., on the planet Altair-4. Commander Adams and the crew of starship C57D have traveled there to search for the survivors of a ship that crashed twenty years before. What they find is Dr. Morbius, his beautiful daughter, Altaira, and a comic robot servant named Robby. (The screenplay, by Cyril Hume, is in part modeled on Shakespeare's *The Tempest* — Morbius is Prospero, Robby Ariel, and Altaira Miranda.)[6] Morbius has discovered the remains of an extinct civilization, the Krell, which had carried technology to its limit. The interior of the planet is one vast machine the purpose of which, Morbius learns, is to materialize one's desires instantaneously. This machine, resembling Frankenstein's laboratory blown up to immense proportions, clearly symbolizes the end to which technology itself strives — the granting of limitless power to man. Morbius plans to keep that power for himself, dispensing bits of the Krell knowledge to humanity when he deems them ready. In order to boost his already elevated IQ, he hooks himself up to the machine. Too late, he finds out why the Krell vanished in a single night. In giving their conscious minds infinite power, the Krell had forgotten about their subconscious hatreds — the machine gave birth to a planet of invisible monsters. Morbius' own Caliban, his "Monster from the Id" empowered by the machine, had killed all the other members of the crew and now roams the planet, threatening Commander Adams' crew and even his own daughter, who has defied his wishes.

At the end of the film, Morbius barricades himself behind massive steel doors with the spaceship crew and watches his monster slowly tear its way through his elaborate technological defenses. Shouting, "My evil self is at the door and I have no way to stop it!" he allows the crew to escape, finds the familiar destruct lever, and annihilates the entire planet. The last scenes of the film show the exploding planet as a brief burst of light, soon lost in the surrounding infinity of stars. Like Walton and his shipmates in *Frankenstein*, Adams and his crew watch the mutual destruction of scientist and Monster, then head back from the limits of the known world to civilization. In both cases, they bring with them awareness of what awaits a culture that lets its technology grant limitless power without self-knowledge. Perhaps the name — Adams — and his imminent marriage to Morbius' daughter, Altaira (cut from the final print) suggest that with this awareness, mankind can begin again.

The film ends as uncertainly as Mary Shelley's novel or any of the Universal movies. Though *Forbidden Planet* seems far from the dark, relatively compact worlds of Mary Shelley, James Whale, or the numerous directors of the Universal series, it explores the same relationship between science, self, and society. From the films comes the elitist, though well-intentioned doctor, his somewhat inhuman assistant, the self-destructible and fantastic laboratory, and the idea of the Monster as a weapon, awakened from its sleep by the scientist's tinkering. At the same time, *Forbidden Planet* enters the psychological realm of the novel. The result is a film that follows elements of the Frankenstein myth in order to see where our technology is taking us. It is a grim vision, foreshadowed in the mutual destruction of Frankenstein and his Monster on Walton's ship and in the windmill and laboratory of Whale's cinematic landscape. But, as in fifties monster movies generally, the awareness of thermonuclear power has intervened to make the scale and potential for destruction immense and cataclysmic.

CHAPTER VIII

New Blood

...it is of the essence of the scientific spirit to be mercilessly ascetic, to eliminate human enjoyment from our relationship to nature, to eliminate the human senses, and finally to eliminate the human brain...Pure intelligence is thus a product of dying, or at least of becoming mentally insensitive, and therefore is in principle madness.

NORMAN O. BROWN

THROUGH THE MIDFIFTIES, when fantasy and science fiction films carried on the Frankenstein tradition, they emphasized the arrogant, Promethean scientist, who discovers his limitations through his creation. His failure is accompanied by remorse and recognition of his own human frailty, of the danger of trying to become "greater than his nature will allow." The message of *Forbidden Planet,* delivered by Commander Adams after Dr. Morbius has met his Monster from the Id, is that "men are not gods"; the line could stand as an epitaph to the house of Frankenstein, from Victor to his many high-strung, neurotic, and ultimately guilt-ridden cinematic descendants. Two other themes in the Frankenstein tradition tended to be downplayed. While creating his Monster, Victor Frankenstein recalls that he was detached from the "horrors of my secret toil" and "insensible to the charms of nature"; closed off from family, friends, and fiancée, apart from human love and natural beauty, his isolation determined the abominable nature of his creation. At the same time, his Monster making is a kind of substitute sexuality. He goes about it with "unremitting ardor" and an "eagerness which perpetually increased" until, one night, with "an anxiety that almost amounted to agony" he infuses the spark of life into his "child." In the 1931 film, Henry Frankenstein ignores his upcoming wedding and carries his experiment to an explosive climax, while locked in his private tower — the life-giving machine, like the tower itself, is unmistakably phallic. The old Baron in the film hints at this aspect of Frankenstein's activities when he suspects that the "work" that keeps him shut away is really another woman. But these scientists come to regret their actions and, ultimately, reconnect themselves to the world of human feeling around them. The character who carries out his Monster breeding with no remorse, no scruples, no interest in the natural world, and with obvious sexual excitement is Dr. Pretorious, who appears only in the 1935 film. Dr. Niemann in *House of Frankenstein*, and Ygor, display some of these tendencies, but not until the British Hammer films of the late fifties and sixties did Pretorian science return in full force, with a Baron Frankenstein who combined cold detachment with a perversity that turned his Monsters into substitute children and sexual playthings.

Two perfectly awful American films released in 1957 and 1958 stood outside both the Universal and Hammer cycles, though they pointed toward the conception of the scientist that took hold in the next decade. *I Was a Teenage Frankenstein* suffers from the bargain-basement look of the early American-International productions, with a wretched laboratory, cardboard sets, and a Monster wearing a T-shirt and Ivy League slacks. Yet the film grossed over two million dollars, following the formula of the even more lucrative *I Was a Teenage Werewolf*. The new audience for horror was largely adolescent; the old Universal films had, at this time, been released to television and started a teen-age fad. The makers of *I Was a Teenage Frankenstein* simply geared the story to the paying customers. Since American-International films were intended primarily for the drive-in crowd, the Monster is assembled from the corpses of dead hot-rodders. As the title implies,[1] it is itself a teen-ager, given to cruising lovers' lane and ogling young girls. The gruesome detail, tongue-in-cheek humor, and few minutes of color the budget would allow enliven the proceedings somewhat, but the focus of the film is clearly on the father-son relationship of scientist and Monster. Dr. Frankenstein is a caricature of the evil parent; he gets to mouth such lines as "Answer me, you have a civil tongue in your head. I know, I sewed it in there!" The Monster, which ultimately is given a new, good-looking head to match its muscular body, is another portrait of a contemporary stereotype — the misunderstood teen-ager. In a sense, the film is a horror version of *Rebel Without a Cause* (1955). The feeling behind them both is that the father, who has "created" his son, wants to dominate him and live vicariously through him. Dr. Frankenstein, head-hunting with his creature through lovers' lane, displays the sexual jealousy the young attribute to the old. When, at the end of the film, he tries to dismantle the Monster to take it back to Europe, the creature rebels. Preferring the new world of Southern California to the old world of Upper Transylvania, it kills its maker but accidentally electrocutes itself, as the screen goes from black and white to color. *Frankenstein — 1970* (the title is a flimsy attempt to suggest the film is futuristic) is, despite the services of Boris Karloff in his only role as a Frankenstein, an even more shoddy exercise, memorable for only two details — the introduction of a pair of disembodied eyeballs for a cheap shock and the face of the dead Monster. Seen only in the last shot, the features are those of a young Baron Frankenstein. The new Monster-maker seeks, through his creation, to renew his sexual vitality and live again.

The Hammer Frankenstein series, which also began in 1957, was certainly not influenced by either of these two films, though it responded to many of the same considerations in re-interpreting the myth. *The Curse of Frankenstein,* directed by Terence Fisher and starring Peter Cushing and Christopher Lee as maker and Monster, was phenomenally successful and set the pattern for the films that followed. For the next fifteen years, Hammer Studios mined the Frankenstein ore and discovered it turned up gold. The series has as its continuing surface features Peter Cushing, ornate period sets, voluptuous women, and various internal organs, all projected on wide screen and bathed in color. The Hammer films have a very different texture than the Universal films, though they borrow some of the familiar elements, such as hunchback Germanic assistants, brain transplants, and elaborate laboratories. Their affinities with the teen-age films include a focus on gore and an emphasis on the generation gap between creator and monster. But the impact of the Hammer films depends, most of all, upon their most striking original feature — the new interpretation of Baron Frankenstein.

Peter Cushing establishes the character as a classic Gothic villain. It is no coincidence that he resembles Count Dracula; director Fisher and scriptwriter Jimmy Sangster were, at the time, working on Hammer's equally successful Dracula series. Both Frankenstein and Dracula are aristocrats with refined manners and eccentric private tastes who travel from drawing room to torture chamber with little change in demeanor. The conception contrasts strongly with the agonized Frankenstein of the Universal epics, though in some ways it reminds us of Dr. Pretorious. There is something slightly effeminate about Cushing's dandified Baron. He creates his Monsters in tanks of water — a "feminine" method foreshadowed by the homunculi in Pretorious' little bottles. Both enjoy dabbling in what Victor Frankenstein called the "unhallowed damps of the grave"; like him, their "attention was fixed upon every object the most insupportable to the delicacy of human feelings." And Cushing's Baron believes with Pretorious that he can artificially create his own children.

At the same time, he displays a strong masculine drive violently directed, more than once, at the young women around him. Pretorious' fascist intentions are undercut by his comic and excitable nature; Cushing's Frankenstein is, above all, serious and restrained. If momentary success excites him, he never exults; if he is beset by doubts, he never shows them. His single-minded devotion to his work, no matter how many times he fails or how far his results are from his intentions, is the source of his strength and his horror. In each film, the Monster is irrevocably destroyed. But the scientist keeps coming back, sometimes disguised as Dr. Frank, sometimes as Dr. Stein, working quietly in some gaslit laboratory, undeterred by the "little miscalculations" that inevitably botch things up.

The assorted Monsters are of secondary significance in these films. None of them comes close to possessing the individuality and power of Karloff's creature; the film makers wisely avoided trying to emulate his portrayal. Christopher Lee played "The Creature" only once, in *The Curse of Frankenstein*, emphasizing its defective brain and brutal power. In that film, Cushing has obtained a brain by murdering a scientist, though it is damaged inadvertently by his assistant, Paul Krempe. The Monster is animated one night when a lightning bolt starts the equipment; Frankenstein is thus spared the necessity of his presence at the creation and any accompanying emotional display. As Frankenstein enters the room, the creature staggers to its feet, tears the bandages from its face, and immediately tries to strangle its creator. There is no attempt to create pathos or deepen the characterization. During its few brief appearances, the Monster is little more than a destructive menace. After Krempe rescues Frankenstein, the Monster escapes to a forest where it kills a blind man. This dim echo of the novel destroys any sympathy for the Monster, contrasting the sylvan setting with the abominable thing that violates it. When Krempe shoots it through the head and Frankenstein promises to bury it, the audience feels little pity. He, of course, soon revives it, though its brain is more useless than ever. It becomes a grotesque puppet, acting out its creator's evil designs. The Baron uses it to murder a young servant girl he has impregnated; then, in one of the best sequences of the film, he proudly demonstrates to his assistant its ability to follow his simple commands like a badly strung marionette. Finally, the Monster is set ablaze and dissolved in acid, decisively ending any chance for a comeback. The film ends with Frankenstein facing a just punishment — his own mutilation by guillotine.

The next in the series, *The Revenge of Frankenstein* (1958), explains his escape: a deformed prison guard shoves the priest under the guillotine in return for a promised new body. Despite the improbable opening, this film in some ways surpasses its predecessor, adding to Cushing's characterization and introducing a genuine note of pathos. The hunchback's new self seems perfect; we see him gleefully burning his old, twisted body after the operation. But he is brutally beaten a few minutes later by a night watchman. As he reverts to his old form, there is a suggestion of a divine and terrible fate that cannot be negated. He is what he must be; Frankenstein's revolt against God's errors of creation, though possibly justified, is doomed to failure. When the Monster bursts through the window of a fashionable home and confronts Dr. "Stein" crying, "Frankenstein, help me!" we are presented, for the first time since *The Bride of Frankenstein*, with an articulate, pathetic Monster who, like the Monster of the novel, asks its creator to take responsibility for it. (Typically, the sequence is mixed in with some awful business about a chimpanzee that has become a cannibal through brain transplants; in addition to its physical problems, the Monster develops a wholly unnecessary taste for human flesh. Restraint is not one of the virtues of the Hammer series.)

Frankenstein himself is an enigmatic figure; he works in a hospital for the poor, if only to secure a supply of human parts. Although he has his selfish motives, he does try to help his assistant by giving him a new body. When the patients at the hospital discover his true identity, they beat him to death. He has, in a sense, taken the philosophical place of the Monster; we are unsure whether his destruction is inevitable and necessary, or if he and his work should be accepted by the world. This transference of the film's center from monster to creator is made explicit in the last scene. After he dies, his assistant puts his brain in a new body. We see Dr. "Frank" opening another office, succeeding where Ygor has failed, literally becoming his own Monster.

Later Hammer films make no attempt at maintaining continuity. Peter Cushing shows up and, after some preliminary scrounging for parts, rolls up his sleeves and gets to work. Despite the lavish trappings that drape the films, none has the individual style and impact of James Whale's classics. Their greatest significance is collective; memories linger of Cushing's cultured accents and diabolical designs, the inevitable laboratory gore and gismos, well-endowed servant girls parading through the scenes, and disasters that arrive like clockwork. As the series progressed, elements that endeared it to its young audience came to the fore. Frankenstein grew older and more undeniably depraved; the Monsters became younger and more appealing. In *Frankenstein Created Woman* (1967) the "monster" is an ex-*Playboy* centerpiece, Susan Denberg, re-brained and (at least in publicity photos) seemingly raped on the operating table by the dastardly Cushing. In *Frankenstein Must Be Destroyed* (1969), the bumbling Baron casually slices off the head of a passer-by and then gets involved with a pair of young nineteenth-century drug dealers. Male chauvinist that he is, he uses the man for his assistant, and keeps the woman around to "make coffee." In the British version, he rapes her to assert his dominance.

It is to Terence Fisher's credit that he can, at times, transcend the numbing sameness of the Hammer formula. His importance to the series is shown by the unremitting sleaziness of the films he didn't direct, such as *The Evil of Frankenstein* (1964), which combines an unconvincing Monster with an absurd plot revolving around a hypnotist called the Great Zoltan, reminding us of the Universal series at its worst. Fisher's style avoids the expressionist idiom of James Whale, relying on straightforward medium shots, a measured pace, and an uncluttered story line. He returns the myth to a Gothic atmosphere, using the familiar Hammer period sets, the evil Baron, and an undercurrent of sexuality to maintain a Romantic mood of depravity and horror. Hammer films have been criticized for their attention to gruesome detail, but anatomical shock is a traditional surprise in the Gothic bag of tricks. The heroines of the demure Mrs. Radcliffe's novels were, for example, forever pulling aside veils and discovering the most loathsome things, while Matthew Lewis's *The Monk* ends in an orgy of torture that makes the Hammer films themselves seem demure by comparison. At their best the films are polished and entertaining, playing with the emotions hidden behind the scientific culture, just as the Gothic movement explored the morbid nightmare side of Romanticism. No longer is the creation of a monster the core of the film. It is accepted that such things can be done with little trouble. More important is the attitude of the creator, and the motivation that keeps him at it, after all of his experiments have such disastrous consequences. Fisher focuses on the Baron's obsession with the literal separation of body and mind, and the sexuality behind it.

The metaphor for the divorce of thought and feeling is the traditional brain transplant, an operation that shows up in all of the Fisher films, always tied to an exploration of the dimensions of the human personality. Despite his occasional attempts at benevolent surgery, Baron Frankenstein is clearly dangerous and insane. He believes the mind is equal to the self; the result is a compulsion to transplant brains, thus reducing the organs of feeling to interchangeable husks. His detachment from his own body makes it possible for him to rape and murder with equal nonchalance and to have his brain moved from Dr. Stein to Dr. Frank with no complications. Such brain switches never work on anyone else. When he murders a famous scientist in *The Curse of Frankenstein* in order to steal his brain, the Baron believes it is not really murder, since his mind will live again in the Monster's body. Of course, the brain is damaged and his plan is thwarted. As we have seen, he does little better with his assistant in *The Revenge of Frankenstein*, whose new body reverts to the form of his old self. In *Frankenstein Created Woman*, the Baron calls his operation a "soul transplant," but it still fails. Christina, his pinup monster, is given the soul of her dead lover. Instead of the perfect union he anticipates, she is driven to murder and suicide. Finally, in *Frankenstein Must Be Destroyed*, he does his best job to date.

The Monster is barely disfigured, with a line of neat stitches around its skull. Again, the Baron's motives seem admirable; he has saved the life of a fellow doctor by transplanting his brain into a new body, curing him of insanity in the process. (Typically, our reactions to his cure are mixed, since *he* caused the doctor's death.) The Monster visits its wife and tries to convince her that it is really her husband with a new body. Her uncomprehending revulsion points up the hopelessness of Frankenstein's dreams; she will not accept the idea that he is no more than his brain. Frankenstein's denial of the part the body plays in making up the self is, first of all, a denial of death. If the brain can outlive the body then, in the Baron's mind, the self is immortal. But in the process, he must deny feeling and life. He sees man as only matter, reducing existence, to "a dull affair, soundless, scentless, colourless, merely the hurrying of material endlessly, meaninglessly." [2] In trying to move personalities from one body to another, he displays the scientific aspect of his generally fascist attitude; control of the body means, on the largest scale, domination of nature and the external world. Frankenstein's insensitivity to the importance of the senses, the totality of the self, the universe of the body, makes him the Monster and dooms his operations to failure.

The Baron's scientific attitudes are reflected in his aberrant sexuality. He lives at some distance from his own body, in a world of nonbeing and nonfeeling, where intellect is all; that explains his personal coldness and matter-of-fact mutilations. His desire for dominance over the world of the body comes out in his violent rapes and murders. His actions suggest that underneath his calm exterior, he hates the body for its frailty and mortality. Therefore, as he gets older, he becomes more brutal toward his young assistants and creations; like the Gothic villains, or the scientist in the "teen-age" films, he comes to play the evil father, seeking sexual domination and new life through control of the next generation. The Baron's sadistic madness is conveyed most subtly through the pornographic display of internal organs that fills the laboratory scene in each film. His compulsion to manipulate his young victims is suggested by his loving violation of their most private parts, as he works in his secret laboratory, quietly singing a tune.

CHAPTER IX

At the Crossroads

Mythical thought for its part is imprisoned in the events and experiences which it never tires of ordering and re-ordering in its search to find them a meaning.

CLAUDE LÉVI-STRAUSS

Myth is a sentence in a circular discourse, a discourse that is constantly changing its meaning: repetition and variation.

OCTAVIO PAZ

THE SUCCESS of the Hammer films meant that the House of Frankenstein now had two distinct branches. Although they share with Mrs. Shelley's novel the fusion of personal madness with the cultural insanity of misused technology, the style and message in each differs. The Universal films are spare and monochromatic, mixing an offbeat humor with an off-center world derived from German expressionism; scientist and Monster are ambiguous figures, caught between pathos and misdirected passion. Frankenstein and sons, led by scientific curiosity or the need for personal glory, create or revive the Monster, but eventually see the enormity of their blasphemous mistakes. Yet the Monster "can never die"; it is the continuing horror of the films, a moribund menace periodically reenergized into a mindless weapon representing the destructiveness latent in the power of modern technology. In the Hammer films, on the other hand, the scientist is immortal, a pure intellect who outlives his own body and, indeed, tries to create a future where the world of the body is superfluous. He is really the monster; his cultured exterior and moral depravity complement the general atmosphere of lavishness, color, and decadence. Despite the continual disasters, the Baron never feels much of anything but a compulsive need to try again. In both Frankenstein cycles, the Monsters embody the principle that the ends justify the means, though the ends are not the same. While each conception is political in the broadest sense, the Hammer films place the blame for a sterile future squarely on a consciously repressive, sadistic, scientific attitude rather than on noble motives distorted by ignorance and arrogance.

The latest additions to the myth carry forth both of these interpretations. In 1973, NBC and ABC each presented four-hour, two-part television productions purporting to return to the original novel; the next year, two elaborate film satires on *Frankenstein* were made by Paul Morrissey and Mel Brooks. Despite the saturation, there is little redundancy, since each combination of teleplay and movie owes its greatest debt to a different branch of the tradition. This parallel evolution suggests that *Frankenstein* is no longer just one story, but a collection of cultural artifacts and attitudes. The two "faithful" adaptions of the Mary Shelley novel are, indeed, faithful to the two offshoots of the myth, while each director pokes fun at his own Frankenstein. Ultimately, though the latest adaptions share names and situations with the novel and each other, their approaches to the relationship between the self, science, and the future of man are as opposed as hope and despair.

The most elaborate retelling so far is, no doubt, NBC's television movie, *Frankenstein: The True Story*. With performances by Leonard Whiting and James Mason, a published screenplay by Christopher Isherwood and Don Bachardy, an inordinate length, an audacious title, and cameo appearances by Sir Ralph Richardson and Sir John Gielgud, the film poses as a serious return to what the credits call "a classic novel by Mary W. Shelley." The screenplay opens with a rather awkward blending of biography and fiction. Mary Shelley, Byron, Shelley, and a middle-aged Dr. John Polidori are picnicking by a Swiss lake. After a series of stilted introductions ("I am Mary Shelley. Here I sit demurely beside my husband. But in my head is a story of horror and you shall hear it") each member of the group acts out the story under Mary's direction, until all but Polidori are transformed into the characters — Polidori shows up in the drama, but retains his own name. In the televised version, this prologue was replaced with a short educational lecture given by James Mason over the grave of Mrs. Shelley. The intent in either case is obviously to lend an air of respectability to the proceedings; the change is at least an improvement in accuracy, since Polidori was twenty years old and Mary Shelley unmarried when she thought of *Frankenstein*. But the effect is still deceptive, since the film has almost nothing to do directly with the novel. The reproduction clearly owes much more to the Hammer movie myth than to Mary Shelley; its pretentious title and prologue only succeed in deluding anyone who hasn't read the novel and irritating anyone who has.

The violence done to the "true story" commences in the first few minutes. We meet Henry Clerval, Frankenstein's friend. But *he* turns out to be the mad doctor, working in a charity hospital like Peter Cushing in *The Revenge of Frankenstein* with much the same object — an unhindered supply of severed limbs. Frankenstein becomes merely *his* sometimes reluctant assistant, who inherits the equipment when Clerval has a heart attack the night before the experiment! In true Hammer tradition, he borrows Clerval's brain to place in the skull of the Monster. The laboratory itself, though in the attic of an old house in the city, is considerably more elaborate than Victor Frankenstein's bare room. Like the period laboratories of the Hammer films, it is full of ornate and colorful apparatus, and spare human parts — in this case a living arm that takes to crawling around the floor. The method of creation involves a series of huge mirrors focusing "solar power from Heaven." The Promethean overtones are dutifully belabored when Clerval tells Frankenstein the myth and pledges him to "join the brotherhood of Prometheus" and "defy the gods." Frankenstein's fiancée is still around; here she is given the proper British surname of Fanshawe. Her function is to fight with Clerval for Frankenstein; early on, she smashes a resurrected butterfly with a Bible, emphasizing the religious theme with a ponderous thump. (Even this obvious bit of symbolism can't be left alone. Clerval remarks afterward: "The vengeance of the Almighty!") The being they create is given the Hammer designation of "The Creature" and, like many of the monsters from those films, is at first young and beautiful. Instead of abandoning or mistreating it, Frankenstein delights in its looks and cleverness, taking it to the opera, teaching it to talk, and otherwise playing the doting father. When it begins to "reverse itself" to Neanderthalish ugliness (a baffling process lifted from *The Revenge of Frankenstein*) its creator can't stand to look at it. The rejection by its "father" causes the creature to hate itself; half encouraged by Frankenstein, it tries to commit suicide in a spectacular leap off the Dover cliffs.

Part Two opens by recalling a convention from the Universal films. The creature discovers that it cannot die, so it wanders into the woods and an encounter with the "Lacy" family, who survive nearly intact from Mrs. Shelley's novel, with only three letters of their name unaccounted for. As in the novel, the Monster's attempts at friendliness are misunderstood, but instead of merely frightening them off, it kills Felix and abducts Agatha. She escapes its clutches only to run into the path of a stagecoach. The Creature takes what's left of her back to the laboratory, which has since been taken over by its third mad scientist tenant, Dr. Polidori.

Polidori had been hovering at the edges of the action from the start. When he comes stage center, the Hammer philosophy emerges in full force. Polidori enlists Frankenstein to reconstruct the body of Agatha into a second, female Monster. The struggle for dominance between the two scientists takes up the rest of the film, pitting two conceptions of science against one another. Frankenstein, like his ancestors from the Universal films and his namesake from the novel, is beset by doubts and destroyed by remorse. He had been led to Monster making by the death of his brother, William, who this time is drowned while trying to retrieve a treasure chest resting, improbably enough, on the bottom of an English lake. When his attempt to find "power over death" only creates a Monster, he lacks the conviction either to accept or destroy it. He and Polidori are about to dissolve the hypnotized creature in a vat of acid, *Curse of Frankenstein* style, when he is seized by guilt and awakens it. The enraged Monster kills one of their assistants and starts a fire that destroys the laboratory. After barely escaping the flames, Polidori tells Frankenstein,

> Let's hope that thing roasting in there is grateful to you — for giving it life! What a model parent you've been! It pleased you as long as it was pretty. Then you wanted to be rid of it, but someone else had to do it for you! So much for your dainty conscience!

Later, he makes clear his differences with Frankenstein when he gives his own reasons for creating monsters:

> What different futures, yours and mine — yet each will have what he deserves! Only fools like Clerval want vulgar fame.

I shall have the power that works unseen and moves the world! You, alone, Frankenstein — when you read in your newspaper that a monarch has been deposed, that two nations are at war — you will say to yourself, that's the hand of Polidori!

The speech is worthy of Doctor Pretorious or Peter Cushing's Baron Frankenstein — two scientists Polidori resembles in more ways than one. His own methods for creating his monster are an adaption of Pretorious' bottles and Cushing's vats — with the assistance of alchemical apparatus and a group of Chinese servants, he creates a chemical womb and hatches Prima, a flawless woman. The sequence is obviously derived from *The Bride of Frankenstein*, though Polidori's reasons for needing Frankenstein's assistance are different. His line about the "hand of Polidori" is ironic, since his real hands are shriveled into bird claws from chemical burns; most of the time he keeps them encased in padded gloves. He is reduced to directing Frankenstein's surgical ministrations to his artificial womb. The episode combines Pretorious' effeminacy with the Hammer concept of the intellect divorced from the body; in this case Polidori is pure mind, using other hands as instruments for his evil designs.

As in the Hammer films, the beings thus created tend to come apart rather easily. Following a successful debut, Prima literally loses her head at a costume ball in a fight with the Monster who has, of course, survived the fire. The next half-hour or so sees the arrest and release of Frankenstein and the escape of the Creature from a jail cell. This echo from the Universal series is combined with the obligatory child scene. Here, the Monster uses a little girl for a shield. When he drops her off, she calls out, with no motivation whatsoever, "Take me with you!" Finally, everyone boards a ship to the Polar seas and a dim rendezvous with the climax of the novel. Elizabeth is strangled; Polidori is hauled to the top of the

mast by the Creature and zapped to jelly by a fortuitous
thunderbolt. For some reason, heaven has finally intervened
— an event foreshadowed by Polidori's hysterical fear of lightning. Frankenstein and his creation head for the ice fields,
where they reach a reconciliation of sorts. Embracing the
Monster, Frankenstein fires a shot that starts an avalanche
crashing down. In Henry Clerval's voice (it was, after all,
his brain) the Creature tells an "amazed and joyful" creator,
"Well done, Victor," while its face is transformed into "the
Creature as we first saw it: innocent, joyful, beautiful." The
final credits roll and we see the Creature slowly moving its
hand above the ice, gaining strength for a sequel we may
hope never comes.

By now it should be obvious that *Frankenstein: The True
Story* lacks any clear direction or consistency. Themes and
incidents from the myth are thrown together with scant regard for the purpose they serve; symbolism is laid on with a
trowel. The film comes apart as easily as the Monsters, leaving us with little more than a few recognizable fragments.
The one thread that helps hold the movie together is colored
by the relationship between Monster making and sexuality
that we have seen before. As Polidori's "womb" and the fate
of Frankenstein and his once beautiful creature suggest, the
sexuality in this version is homosexuality. Throughout, the
unnatural creation of monsters and the natural creation of
human beings are contrasted. Elizabeth tells Frankenstein,
early on, that they can make life themselves, after marriage.
He replies disdainfully, "So can a pair of animals . . . Why can't
I raise life from death?" After they marry, she discovers that
Victor fears the child they are expecting will be a son and
remind him of his dead brother — evidently natural "resurrection" is intolerable, even though his experiments stem from
a desire to defeat the death that claimed William. Elizabeth
also competes with men for her husband throughout the film.

She says of Clerval, "If I were a man I think I should kill him," while she actually tries to destroy Polidori, whom she calls a "corrupting force," by locking him in his cabin with the Creature.

Both male and female monsters are created in secrecy by a pair of men; Polidori's chemical womb is a momentary triumph for this male fantasy of birth without woman. The emphasis upon the "sin" of these experiments, and their contrast with natural procreation, suggests that the tragedy that overwhelms Frankenstein and his inhuman protégé is more sexual than scientific. At the end of the film, the misshapen child of Frankenstein's unnatural activities meets Elizabeth, who is pregnant with Frankenstein's child:

Elizabeth: What more do you want of him?
Creature: Victor made me.
Elizabeth: God has forgiven him for that sin. He has a child now. *Our* child!
(With instinctive pride, she places her hand on her body)
Creature: (Seemingly dismayed) Child?
(It reaches out to touch Elizabeth's body. She steps back with instant revulsion)

Unfortunately, the subtlety of the theme is lost in the baroque and illogical excesses of the production. Caught between pretensions of "seriousness" and literary accuracy and a large unacknowledged debt to the inherently tongue-in-cheek and derivative film tradition, *Frankenstein: The True Story* is disunified and unconvincing. Like the Creature itself, it is controlled by too many diverse masters ever to have a life of its own.

Excess is the technique of Paul Morrissey in *Andy Warhol's Frankenstein* (Warhol's name is mainly for publicity purposes); by reproducing the hues and undertones of the Hammer brand of horror in garish detail, Morrissey achieves effective if stomach turning parody. His methods include both color and 3–D — a flashy process that, paradoxically, subtracts from the realism of the proceedings. The audience's first impression is of a miniature, Easter-egg landscape (carefully accentuated by the opening shots of a picturesque pony cart). Gradually, as the film becomes less innocent, we are drawn into that world. When the effects work, they can be quite remarkable; too often, however, the 3–D images are fuzzy or out of register. The technological counterfeit of "realism" keeps the viewer at a distance and makes the sadism more acceptable, while providing an easy escape — when things got too grisly many members of the audience removed their glasses and transformed the butchery into an eye-wrenching blur.

The gore itself is gruesomely detailed. The beheadings in the Hammer films and *The True Story* are recalled with a vengeance. This Baron, played with a gutteral accent and sadistic leer by Udo Kier, snips off a head with a giant shears. The camera lingers on the quivering torso spurting blood and the still twitching face. More than half in love with death, Frankenstein and his bug-eyed assistant make explicit the sexuality behind their obsessions. They waylay their victim returning from a brothel, as the Baron ineffectually conceals his phallic scissors under his coat. Later, Frankenstein rapes the half-completed female creature on the operating table; his assistant inadvertently disembowels it when he mistakes a scar for its sexual organs. The confusion of sex and death is the source of much of the "comedy"; like Cushing's Baron, this Frankenstein finds fulfillment in violation of the body, though he goes about it with undisguised directness.

Through these scenes, Morrissey is violating our outer shell of respectability, testing the limits of our tolerance, and playing with the sexual appeal of violence that keeps the audience peering through its fingers at the action. The popularity of the film, and violently explicit films like it, may show us how far our culture has entered the forbidden realm that is the province of the Hammer Frankensteins. In such a world, the Baron's incestuous relationship with his sister seems almost normal and is, in fact, mentioned offhandedly. Morrissey's comment on the nature of the new pornography of violence is visualized in one deft touch: although Frankenstein's sexual tastes are, to put it kindly, depraved, he is careful to keep the sexual organs of his monsters decorously covered.

A few scenes suggest the political implications of a Pre-torian "new world of gods and monsters." Frankenstein builds his creatures in a laboratory decorated with Greek statuary and elegantly draped anatomical parts, as classical music plays in the background. He is an aristocrat; like his wife, he seeks young and presumably virile peasants for his diversions. The aim is a familiar one — to mate his monsters and become god and father to a new race. When he finally unveils his crea-tions to his shrewish sister-wife and her peasant lover, the monsters are wearing leather collars, braces, and fashionable clothing. With few words of explanation, the company sits down to dinner at a long candelabra-bedecked table. As the collection of misfits engage in the usual idle chatter, the scene slowly fades to darkness. Frankenstein's cultured madness promises a tasteful tyranny — a love of the beauty of things stripped of their human significance. What goes on behind the laboratory doors is of no interest to Frankenstein's wife, who has a mildly perverse private life of her own. As long as the social amenities are observed, each is allowed his little quirks.

The Baron is father to more than his monsters. He has a pair of Nordic children who spy on their parents' secret lives, practicing dissections on their dolls. When, at the end, they are confronted with the peasant hero trussed up over the dead bodies of their father, mother, and the two monsters, they know what to do. The credits unroll as they take out Daddy's scalpels and slowly winch up their victim to slitting position. The next generation of Frankensteins has learned by example that life and death are as interchangeable as human limbs, heads, and organs. The same conclusion had been reached by the male Monster, who answered his friend's desperate pleading, "It's better to breathe than not to breathe" by casually ripping out the stitches that loosely hold it together and joining the pool of entrails on the floor.

Everyone is easily dismembered, from the monsters barely held together by their leather braces, to the Baron himself, who loses his hand in a chase with the Monster, then throws it at his pursuer. He gives his last speech facing us with a spear run through him and his liver hanging on the point, suspended in 3–D over an audience that simultaneously titters and squirms. Like the Hammer films and *The True Story*, *Andy Warhol's Frankenstein* derives much of its impact from an emphasis upon the frailty of the body — the childhood fear that if we can easily pull the stuffing out of our teddy bear, someone can do the same to us. The images of dismemberment are, as well, a kind of castration, aptly expressing the sterility at the core of the sexuality displayed in these films. As might be expected, the Monster the Baron creates to start a new race turns out to be impotent. No one in the film really feels much of anything. The hero is played by Joe Dellasandro, an actor notorious for his inability to convey any emotion in even the most passionate scenes. The children of the Baron who prepare to cut up their first victim have inherited a world in which the body has no more integrity than a fragile doll and the soul is nonexistent.

The scientists in all these films are mad puppet masters who work in an amoral vacuum, with the power to disassemble what they have created when it no longer pleases them. This vision of the scientific future is pornographic and devoid of redeeming social values. Morrissey's laughter is directed at the fact that what he shows us can be seen by a mass audience as comic. The use of 3–D only demonstrates more clearly that the audience, like the scientists, has the capacity to detach itself from the human significance of the proceedings when they are presented through the "sanitizing" technological medium. The same thing happened in the novel during the construction of the Monster, when Frankenstein could "procrastinate his feelings of affection" in order to "torture the living animal to animate the lifeless clay." The impression that comes from the Hammer branch of the myth is that we all may be losing ourselves in that cold world, beyond the limits imposed by human warmth and feeling, where life is no more than animate matter.

A very different version of Mary Shelley's novel came to television the same year as *The True Story*. The Dan Curtis production of *Frankenstein* was shown on two successive nights in 1973 as part of ABC's *Wide World of Entertainment* series. Written by Sam Hall and Richard Landau, the play is the closest adaption of the novel to date, compressing the geography of the book while keeping the names and personalities of all but the Monster reasonably intact. However, it is the novel seen through the myth; the Universal films lend props, situations, and a philosophical approach that take us away from the world of the Hammer films and reorder the universe of Mary Shelley.

The build-up until the creation of the Monster is straight from James Whale's first film. The only additions to Mary Shelley's cast of characters are Otto and Hans, undeformed members of filmdom's lineage of Germanic laboratory assistants. They join Frankenstein for a traditional bit of grave robbing, then help him adjust the apparatus, which includes the usual melange of copper wires and electrodes, along with a lightning rod "capable of being extended through an opening in the roof." The process involves the standard Universal electrical storm — Frankenstein even paraphrases Colin Clive when he tells Otto, "The storm will be overhead soon. Quickly, make sure everything is secure!" When Elizabeth, his father, Alphonse, and Henry Clerval arrive as the experiment is about to begin, we are reminded of the equally untimely arrival of Elizabeth, the old Baron, and Victor Moritz over forty years before.

Strangely enough, none of the Hammer style *Frankensteins* uses a thunderstorm to create the Monster, though a lightning bolt accidentally begins the process in *The Curse of Frankenstein* and solar energy provides the power in *The True Story*. The Hammer scientists generally ignore the natural world, though it can intrude accidentally or provide a source of energy. In the Whale films, as in the television *Frankenstein*, nature holds awesome, cataclysmic power which can merely be tapped by science, only at the proper moment, and with great personal danger. Each conception owes something to the novel. The Hammer methods are faithful to the isolation of the original Victor Frankenstein from the world of nature, while Universal's Gothic thunderstorm both recalls the rain that "pattered dismally against the panes" of Victor Frankenstein's attic room and the lightning bolt that splintered the tree in front of his home and showed him the destruction latent in his brief command of the "spark of life." In the ABC *Frankenstein*, the thunderbolt returns as the instrument that both creates and destroys the Monster's mate on the operating table. Unsure whether to give his second creature life, Frankenstein in effect lets nature decide for him. Throughout the production, though he copies the methods of Colin Clive, Robert Foxworth's scientist is a much more sympathetic character, a Monster maker who could, at many moments, have been led from the path that brought his predecessors to "utter and terrible destruction."

144

This Victor Frankenstein is no Pretorian madman. We first see him delivering his "Volingen Prize" paper to an audience at Ingolstadt University. His lecture on the possibility of using science to extend life is greeted with cries of "heresy" and "blasphemy," culminating in a mass walkout. He seems to be presented almost as an heroic figure, a scientific pioneer on a par with Freud or Galileo. His vision, however, is clouded by arrogance. When Waldman warns that "others must be led gradually into new ways of thinking" he brushes his old teacher off with a smile. We soon learn that he will test his theories that night, giving life to the Monster that will eventually destroy him. Throughout the play, we get the impression that Frankenstein might have succeeded in conquering death, if he had listened to Waldman, gone slowly, and heeded his teacher's concern for the "moral implications of such work." The possibilities are conveyed by the Galilean image of the telescope, which shows up twice early in the drama. Frankenstein has used the brain of a scientist whose hobby had been astronomy, and gives the newly awakened Monster a toy telescope to stir its memories. Instead, it mindlessly crushes the instrument. Later that night, after it kills Otto, Frankenstein fakes his death by throwing the body off a ledge and making it appear that he had leaned out too far while looking through another telescope. The point is made: vision without understanding or restraint is disastrous.

The difference between this *Frankenstein* and its cinematic ancestors is suggested by Frankenstein's concern over the one missing part he still needs. The night of the creation, he and his assistants head for a graveyard to steal a human heart. When Hans is shot, Frankenstein is ready to abandon his experiment and risk detection by sending for a doctor. He is dissuaded by Hans, who pleads that the experiment go on and makes a last bequest of his own heart. Frankenstein's very human emotions here, as throughout the drama, are underscored by the emphasis upon the heart, and not the brain. He is not a representative of a purely intellectual, amoral science, but a fallible individual who, like Mary Shelley's scientist, allows his own heart to lead him into an icy region of death. The mood is deepened by the character of his other assistant, Otto. Otto serves the function of Fritz in the 1931 film, but he is neither twisted nor demented. An intelligent and sensitive individual, he at first tries to stop the experiment, saying, "I think we've already gone too far," but then helps animate the Monster. Like Fritz, Otto expresses directly the hidden emotions of his master, but in this case they are a blend of doubt, arrogance, and eagerness.

The Monster itself is Karloffian in conception — a giant, scarred hulk — though its innocence receives greater stress. Even before its creation it is associated with childhood. Frankenstein, Hans, and Otto celebrate the Volingen Prize with paper hats and toys, including a large ball, in the laboratory the day before the experiment. The creature, which is called "The Giant," takes its first steps "like a toddler"; Otto calls it, "A baby! A giant baby!" Otto and Victor are proud parents, using children's games to teach the Monster language and coordination. But the Giant is a baby with superhuman strength, whose joy can turn to childlike rage in an instant. Soon after the creation, Otto and the Giant play ball, until Otto says, "We've other things to do." It responds by commanding, "Play ... Otto!" with a voice that is "harsher" and a face that wears a "ferocious expression." Otto agrees and, in its happiness, the Giant hugs him to death. When Frankenstein returns, the Giant is bouncing the ball at Otto's crushed body, repeating, "Play ... Otto ... play" without comprehension.

The ambivalence we feel throughout the drama toward the Giant is conditioned by this unnatural juxtaposition of power and innocence. Whenever we see children playing with the

Monster nearby (and the scene is repeated) the suggestion is that it may join in and inadvertently use its power to kill. Once, it cradles a bird in its hand and accidentally squeezes the life out of it; later, William Frankenstein is kind to it, and it breaks his neck while trying to keep him from calling out. The philosophical ambiguity of Mary Shelley's Monster is effectively paralleled, here as in Whale's first film, by the dangerous innocence of the creature. We feel quite sympathetic toward its loneliness and are moved by its hunger for love. For example, when hiding by the De Lacey cottage, it makes a crude doll from a stick of wood and holds pathetic conversations with it. But, after the death of William, when it is protesting to the doll, "I didn't hate him...I couldn't help myself," the stage directions note, "Unconsciously, his hands crush the puppet and it crumbles to bits in his hands." This power, so easily unleashed, makes the Giant a Monster in spite of itself. All of its accidental murders of children remind us of Karloff's famous scene with the little girl by the lake. In both films, the danger from the Monster is a product of its murderous strength and undeveloped brain. The Monsters think like machines or infants. Karloff's creature reasons crudely — if the flowers float, the girl will float. The Giant is unable to combine strong feelings with gentle actions. Its rage, fear, even its love, are immediately translated into crushing physical force. The relationship to technology is obvious; what the monsters lack our machines lack. The same combination of primitive "reasoning" and superhuman power makes them potentially just as dangerous.

The second half of the story closely follows the events of the novel. The Giant tears down the De Lacey cottage, convinces Frankenstein to build a mate which is destroyed on the operating table, and vows to be with its maker on his wedding night. The differences are, again, in the character of the Monster, whose determination to revenge itself on its maker is un-accompanied by the "hellish triumph" felt by Mary Shelley's Monster. We believe it when it tells Frankenstein it killed Elizabeth with the greatest reluctance, for it continually tries to reestablish a bond of feeling with its creator. Once, when Frankenstein removes a bullet from its arm, it tells him, "I have all the hurt of the world inside me. You can't give me any more."

At the end of the drama, they meet in a modest equivalent of the icebound region near the North Pole — the mist-shrouded ruins of an ancient spa. After Frankenstein falls and is impaled on a spike, the Giant takes him in its arms. Frankenstein and Monster beg each other for forgiveness; in a last moment of childlike discovery, the Giant sheds tears and joyfully says, "I cry . . . I cry." Though they both die (the Giant intentionally draws the fire of the pursuing villagers) Frankenstein and Monster find a happiness denied their earlier counterparts. They escape the icy universe of nonfeeling which is the destination of Mary Shelley's characters and the domain of the Hammer Frankensteins; the play closes with them covered in mist "like a shroud," united in death as, "for the first time, there is full peace on both their faces." The ending is superficially similar to the conclusion of *The True Story*, but there is a deeper difference. The union is not a hopeless personal one, or merely a device that ends one story and prepares for a resurrection in another. It is, instead, a declaration of faith that a reconciliation between man and his creations is possible. It has been implied all along that Frankenstein's experiment was not sinful in itself. He should, however, have taken into account the fears of those he scorned and the feelings of that he created, if there ever was to be a happier ending.

In order to hold out that possibility, the makers of the ABC *Frankenstein* had to beg one of the important questions of the novel. Mary Shelley's Monster is so abominable no human can overcome his natural revulsion long enough to offer it acceptance and love. The Giant, played by Bo Svenson, a huge blond Swede, is described as hideous but is made up to look only mildly monstrous. If the Giant is, nevertheless, a symbol for a dangerously flawed technology, and Frankenstein a representative of imprudent science, then this retelling of the myth concludes with hope for the future. Neither has been left beyond the reach of human feeling; their emotions are the source of success, disaster, and a last communion. The indication is that, led in the right direction, the new science and its ungainly child could learn to live together.

This hope is finally realized at the end of Mel Brooks' *Young Frankenstein* (1974), when creator and creature each marry and settle into happy domesticity. Mel Brooks claims to have read Mary Shelley's *Frankenstein* carefully and taken it seriously; he obviously has an intimate feeling for the great Universal films of the thirties. Shot in nostalgic black and white, *Young Frankenstein* is replete with archaic devices, such as the iris and wipe shots that mark the transition between scenes, as well as little touches familiar to lovers of the old Frankenstein movies. Ygor's truncated walking stick, Inspector Kemp's wooden arm, the Caligariesque village, and the cobwebbed castle are only a few of the details that make the film a visual retrospective. The principals even act in the grand manner. Gene Wilder does a splendid imitation of Colin Clive, Basil Rathbone, et al., at their most frenetic, while Peter Boyle's sensitive interpretation of the Monster, in Karloffian make-up by William Tuttle, rivals that of the great Boris himself. At the same time, the characters pay homage to Mary Shelley, quoting directly from her novel, here called *How I Did It,* by Victor Frankenstein. But Brooks does not borrow from the past merely to mock it. Although a satire, all concerned show respect for the tradition — they never let on that they take the proceedings as anything but real. The film sets out quite deliberately to remake the entire myth and bring it to a comic conclusion. Brooks's film is diametrically opposed to the sardonic sadism of Morrissey's *Andy Warhol's Frankenstein;* infused by a genuine love for the old Monsters and faith in human nature, Mel Brooks tries, once and for all, to transform the horror tale into a fairy tale, and let maker and monster live happily ever after.

The title suggests his approach. *Young Frankenstein* is a cinematic Bildungsroman; Frederick Frankenstein, grandson of Victor, comes to maturity by coming to terms with his own past. At the beginning of the film, we see him lecturing on the dissection of the brain at Baltimore General Hospital. He is a representative modern scientist, parodying the detached scientific method when he uses an old man to demonstrate the action of the central nervous system. After Frankenstein kicks him in the groin while cursing in his ear, the patient is wheeled out, doubled over in pain, as the good doctor tells his assistant, "Give him an extra dollar." When a student asks about his grandfather, Frankenstein explodes into an hysterical denial of any but an "accidental relationship to a famous cuckoo." He even denies his family name, insisting it be pronounced "Fronk-en-steen." His actual deep connections with his ancestors are exposed when, with manic vehemence, he emphasizes his rejection of the past by driving a scalpel into his leg. In a way, Frankenstein's personal reaction to his lineage parallels the suppression by modern science of the questions raised in the Frankenstein myth. Frederick insists that since the central premise — the creation of life — is impossible, the story itself has no significance. When, after his lecture, he is presented with his great-grandfather's legacy, he is forced to travel to Transylvania and there relive his past and face the Monster.

The precreation scenes are handled brilliantly. At the railroad station, Frederick meets his beautiful laboratory assistant, Inga, and Igor's grandson (who pronounces his own name "Eye-gor"). Together they travel to the family castle, a Gothic pile complete with scurrying rats, forbidding stone staircases, and a stone-faced housekeeper, Frau Blucher. That night, Frankenstein awakens from a nightmare, chanting, "Destiny, destiny, no escaping that for me!" Drawn by violin music to his grandfather's secret library, he reads Mary Shelley's creation scene from Victor's book and immediately decides, "It Could Work!" Borrowing a body from the gallows, he adds a brain stolen by Igor from the "brain depository" (of course, as Igor later admits, "It's from someone named 'A. B. Normal'"). The James Whale creation scene is staged using the original Strickfaden apparatus. As maker and Monster ascend to the roof together, Frankenstein extends his arms in a crucifixion pose which casts a huge shadow on the wall, and exults in the resurrection of his grandfather's madness.

Soon after the creation comes to life, it escapes, and Frederick laments, "Oh God in Heaven, what have I done?" He manages with considerable difficulty to subdue the Monster with a sedative (as in Whale's first film) and lock it in a small stone room. Here *Young Frankenstein* and its sources diverge. Rather than abandon the Monster, Frederick decides to enter alone and win it over. He tells the others to ignore his pleas to be let out, adding, "Love is the only thing that can save this poor creature, and I am going to convince him that he is loved, even at the cost of my own life." At first, of course, he screams to be released, pleading, "I was joking! Don't you know a joke when you hear one?" Then he calls for "Mommy!" The scene is the most important in the film; Frederick is really facing his own past and his own self, trying to work through his fear to love. When he realizes he can't escape, he turns from the door to tell the Monster, "You are not evil; you are good." As it starts to sob, he hugs it and continues, "This is a nice boy, this is a good boy, this is a mother's angel . . . I want the world to know once and for all and without any shame that we love him!" By conquering his own creation with love, he can accept his own self and undo the curse that hangs over the house of Frankenstein. His new understanding is shown when Inga asks, through the door, "Dr. Fronk-en-steen, are you all right?" He screams back triumphantly, "MY NAME IS FRANKENSTEIN!"

The suggestion that the Monster is linked to its maker is underscored in the next scene when both appear identically dressed in top hat and tails to perform "Puttin' on the Ritz." The Monster's debut before a paying audience stirs memories of *King Kong* and results in a similar debacle. Frederick Frankenstein has done better than any of his predecessors in taming the Monster, but he still thinks like Carl Denham, who presented Kong as "The Eighth Wonder of the World" and a vehicle for his own triumph. While locked in the room, Frederick told the Monster that together, they "would make the greatest single contribution to science since the creation of fire" and here, before the performance, he treats it like the old man in the lecture room, showing off the refinements of its nervous system and its ability to obey simple commands while rewarding it like a trained seal. In *King Kong*, the monster is frightened by popping flash bulbs; in *Young Frankenstein*, an exploding footlight accomplishes the same thing. When they are unable to pick up the tempo for the final chorus, Frederick cries, "For God's sake, come on! Are you trying to make me look like a fool! I will not let you destroy my work . . . as your creator I command you to come back!" The Monster lurches off into the night, while Frankenstein is left with the knowledge that he has not yet found the way to make peace with his creation.

The answer had been before him all along. Throughout the film, the two emotions of fear and love presented to the

Monster are symbolized by fire and music. The first time the Monster escapes, it wanders into a series of parodies of famous scenes from the Whale films. It meets the little girl and the hermit but leaves them both unharmed, killing only a sadistic guard who torments it with fire. When the burning footlight, the villagers' fear, and Frankenstein's megalomanic commands frighten off the Monster again, it is drawn back to the castle, as always, by violin music. Frau Blucher had first used the violin to lure Frederick into repeating his grandfather's experiment. After the creation, she releases the Monster, while Frederick and Igor cringe in terror. She shows them the power music has "to reach the soul when words are useless"; as she plays the violin, the creature Frankenstein called a "seven-and-a-half-foot long, fifty-four-inch-wide gorilla" pathetically tries to grasp the notes from the air. At the same time, she reveals that Victor Frankenstein was once her "boyfriend." Her awareness of the power of love teaches her how to tame the Monster and reform Frederick Frankenstein. When he locks himself in the room with his creation, Frau Blucher is the only one who helps him, by preventing the others from letting him out too soon. Her violin theme, heard from the opening moments of the film to its final fadeout, is a continual reminder of the redeeming power of love.

The "power of love" has other, more direct, manifestations. The sexual prowess of the Monster, used for a lot of laughs, is also one clue to the meaning Victor's creation holds for its creator. Frederick is sexually frustrated; his fiancée, Elizabeth, who joins him at the castle near the end of the film, rarely lets him touch her and is careful to warn, "No tongues!" before they kiss. Monster making is, again, substitute sexuality; he makes love with Inga on the operating table, describes the creation itself as an attempt to "penetrate the very womb of impervious Nature," and emphasizes that his creature will have what she calls "an enormous schvannschtuker." After Elizabeth has sent a grunting Frederick off to bed in his own room, the grunting Monster breaks in and does what Frankenstein is obviously fantasizing — it carries her off and rapes her. We discover its sexual powers are magical; as Elizabeth is raped, she begins singing, "Ah, sweet mystery of life, at last I've found you!" But love is the stronger charm; the Monster is called away from the now compliant Elizabeth by the music. Frankenstein entices it back to the castle in order finally to make it "as right as rain." The second time he risks his life, his motives are untarnished by hopes of scientific glory, and he succeeds. Frankenstein transfers part of his brain to the Monster and receives its most prominent part in return.

The exchange makes clear what Frankenstein has discovered by reliving the myth. He and the Monster become one, while each gets what he needs to complete himself. Frankenstein learns that intellect without love means failure; the Monster gives up some of its sexual power in order to gain, in its own words, "a calmer brain and a somewhat more sophisticated way of expressing myself." The Monster is, on one level, the shadow of Frederick Frankenstein, the side he feared and repressed. By learning to love that part of himself, he gains its magic, accepts his own past, and changes the future. The Monster receives the wisdom, direction, and love necessary to make it human. This same recognition of our affinities with the Monster is pointed up when Inspector Kemp bursts in with the villagers just as the cure is nearing completion. After the Monster rises from the table and startles everyone by telling them of its rehabilitation, Kemp replies, "This is, of course, an entirely different situation. As the leader of this community, may I be the first to offer my hand in friendship." Since Kemp, like Inspector Krogh in *Son of Frankenstein*, has a wooden arm, the Monster takes him at his word and tears it off. We remember that Kemp, like the Monster, has trouble being understood when he speaks and is partly artificial. The scene shows us everyone accepting the Monster among them and within them. The villagers, who have been "threatened five times before," will finally have nothing to worry about from the house of Frankenstein.

Mel Brooks leaves the Monster in bed reading the *Wall Street Journal*. It has married Elizabeth, who has miraculously sprouted an Elsa Lanchester hairdo from *The Bride of Frankenstein*, and now slinks to bed, hissing merrily at her "old zipper neck." Frankenstein has married Inga, and waits, grunting eagerly, to unveil to his bride what the Monster has given him. As is often the case in the traditional Bildungsroman, marriage concludes the adventure, and shows us that the hero has finally reached sexual and emotional maturity. The ending fulfills the expectations of all of us who have always had a place in our hearts for the Karloff Monster and hoped, in one film at least, that it could find peace. At the same time, *Young Frankenstein* portrays an end to the conflict between science, technology, and society. Earlier, while preparing to make Frederick "curse the day he was born a Frankenstein" the villagers curse scientists in general, who "say they're working for us, when what they really want is to rule the world!" The film argues that, through an understanding of the Frankenstein myth, such fears can be eliminated. Frederick learns, as Mary Shelley indicated, that our technology reflects ourselves and our motives; if we replace repression, fear, arrogance, and the desire for control with acceptance, love, humility, and the capacity for understanding, our machines can become a well-adjusted part of our culture.

Young Frankenstein and *Andy Warhol's Frankenstein* present two violently opposed visions of who we are and what we may be creating. Mel Brooks domesticates and humanizes our technology; Paul Morrissey reduces man to a machine. Each director may have thought his version definitive, but the myth of Frankenstein, which began with the Industrial

Revolution, will continue to evolve as long as there are machines and men to make them. Mrs. Shelley ended her novel in midjourney; these two films are but two possible destinations. The distance between them is less extreme than it seems, since they are connected by the insight first expressed in Mary Shelley's remarkable novel and present in the many permutations of the myth. In seeking to coexist with our technological Monster, we must remember that its grip on life is tenacious, its arguments for acceptance compelling, and its potential for destruction boundless. It is a magnified image of ourselves.

Notes

A Selected Chronology of
Frankenstein Films

A Guide to Further Reading

Index

Notes

PROLOGUE

1. The Living Theatre production of *Frankenstein* is described in Renfreu Neff, *The Living Theatre: USA* (New York. Bobbs-Merrill, 1970), pp. 61–72; the quotation is from L. Sprague De Camp, *Science Fiction Handbook* (New York: Hermitage House, 1953), p. 42.

2. Although Polidori's story, *The Vampyre*, has recently been remembered as one source for Bram Stoker's *Dracula*.

3. All references to *Frankenstein* are from Mrs. Shelley's final, 1831 version, edited by M. K. Joseph (London: Oxford University Press, 1969).

4. Walton's destination helps establish *Frankenstein* as a precursor of modern science fiction since, in the early eighteenth century, the unexplored Polar regions were the locus of the type of fantasies that would later populate the planets of the science fiction universe.

5. Critics of *Frankenstein* have often hinted at the strange connection between creator and Monster, without making much of it. Richard Church, in *Mary Shelley* (New York: Viking, 1928), writes that they are two halves of a single being, while Muriel Spark, in *Child of Light* (Hadleigh, Essex: Tower Bridge, 1951), rather simplistically contends that Frankenstein is pure emotion and the Monster pure intellect. Harold Bloom, in "*Frankenstein*, or the New Prometheus," *Partisan Review*, 32 (1965), pp. 611–18, mentions the concept of the shadow as part of a "very complex" antithesis; Lowry Nelson, Jr., in "Night Thoughts on the Gothic Novel," *Yale Review*, 52 (1962), pp. 236–57, says both characters are "objectified parts of single personality" and Masao Miyoshi,

159

in *The Divided Self* (New York: NYU Press, 1969), calls the Monster the "scientist's deviant self." Yet no one has attempted a thoroughgoing analysis of the relationship or linked it to the themes of the novel.

6. See, for example, Christopher Small, *Mary Shelley's "Frankenstein": Tracing the Myth* (Pittsburgh: University of Pittsburgh Press, 1973).

CHAPTER ONE

1. *Mary Shelley's Journal*, ed. Frederick L. Jones (Norman: University of Oklahoma Press, 1947), p. 23.
2. Sylva Norman, "Mary Wollstonecraft Shelley," in *Shelley and His Circle*, Vol. XIII. ed. Kenneth Neil Cameron (Cambridge: Harvard University Press, 1970), p. 399. One of the best of the many biographies available is Elizabeth Nitchie, *Mary Shelley: Author of "Frankenstein"* (New Brunswick: Rutgers University Press, 1953).
3. The visitor was Hartley Coleridge, and his comment is quoted in Mary G. Lund, "Mary W. Shelley and the Monster," *University of Kansas City Review*, 27 (1962), p. 253. His father, Samuel T. Coleridge, wrote in a letter to Robert Southey in 1799 that "... the cadaverous Silence of Godwin's Children is to me quite catacomb-ish..." (*Collected Letters of S. T. Coleridge*, ed. Earl L. Griggs, Vol. I [London: Oxford University Press], p. 305).
4. Eileen Bigland, *Mary Shelley* (London: Cassell, 1959), p. 33.
5. Norman, p. 399. Elizabeth Nitchie quotes an unpublished letter of Mary Shelley's in which she writes of her father, "Until I met Shelley I [could?] justly say he was my God — and I remember many childish instances of the [ex]cess of attachment I bore for him" (p. 89).
6. *Journal*, p. 207.
7. Nitchie, p. 9.
8. Nitchie, p. 8.
9. *Journal*, p. 185.
10. *The Letters of Mary Shelley*, Vol. I, ed. Frederick L. Jones (Norman: University of Oklahoma Press, 1946), p. 216.
11. *Letters*, I, p. 233.
12. Mary Shelley's self-revelation in *Frankenstein* is supported by her lifelong tendency to draw self-portraits in her writing. For exam-

ple, a short story published in 1836, "The Parvenue," is "clearly drawn from her pent-up feelings of inferiority and imposition derived from her years as Shelley's mistress, wife, and widow, and as the dutiful daughter of Godwin" (Burton Pollin, "Mary Shelley as the Parvenue," *Review of English Literature [Leeds]*, 8 [1967], p. 20.) In 1819, she wrote *Mathilda*. According to its modern editor, Elizabeth Nitchie, "not even her worst enemy could say harsher things about Mary than Mary says about herself in the obviously autobiographical *Mathilda*" ([Chapel Hill: University of North Carolina Press, 1959], p. 11). One reason this novel was never published in Mrs. Shelley's lifetime is that the heroine's father confesses incestuous desires for his daughter. This bit of wish-fulfillment (if that's what it was) proved too strong for nineteenth-century publishers; the novel was found among Mrs. Shelley's papers at her death in 1851.

13. *Letters*, II, p. 250.
14. Nitchie, p. 23.
15. *Letters*, II, p. 98.
16. Ernest J. Lovell, Jr., "Byron and the Byronic Hero in the Novels of Mary Shelley," *Studies in English (University of Texas)*, 30 (1951), pp. 165, 183. Oddly enough, neither Lovell nor W. E. Peck, in his lengthy study of "The Biographical Element in the Novels of Mary Wollstonecraft Shelley," (*PMLA*, 38 [1923] pp. 196–219) makes any mention of *Frankenstein*.
17. In Ellen Moer's excellent article "Female Gothic: The Monster's Mother," *New York Review of Books*, 21 (March 21, 1974), pp. 24–28.
18. In Samuel Rosenberg, "*Frankenstein*, or Daddy's Little Monster," *Confessions of a Trivialist* (Baltimore: Penguin Books, 1972).

CHAPTER TWO

1. He is clearly also cast in the image of Shelley. In her preface to the 1824 edition of his poetry, Mary Shelley described her husband in words that could be applied to Clerval: "...his fearless enthusiasm in the cause which he considered the most sacred upon earth, the improvement of the moral and physical state of mankind, was the chief reason why he...was pursued by hatred and calumny. No man was more devoted than he to the endeavour of making those around him happy; no man ever pos-

sessed friends more unfeignedly attached to him." (P. B. Shelley, *Complete Poetical Works*, ed. Thomas Hutchinson [London: Oxford University Press, 1961], p. xiii). She could be speaking of Shelley when, in the novel, Frankenstein says of Clerval, "Excellent Friend! how sincerely did you love me, and endeavour to elevate my mind until it was on a level with your own."

2. J. A. Hadfield, *Dreams and Nightmares* (Baltimore: Penguin Books, 1954), p. 188.
3. *Journal*, p. 170.
4. Spark, p. 129.

CHAPTER THREE

1. *Letters of Edward John Trelawny*, ed. H. Buxton Forman (1910; rpt. New York: Amis Press, 1973), p. 194.
2. Mrs. Julian Marshall, *Life and Letters of Mary W. Shelley* (London: R. Bentley & Sons, 1889), Vol. II, 266.
3. Mario Praz, *The Romantic Agony* (London: Oxford University Press, 1970), p. 116.
4. Philip Wade, "Influence and Intent in the Prose Fiction of Percy and Mary Shelley," Diss. North Carolina, 1966, p. 77.
5. See James Rieger, "Dr. Polidori and the Genesis of Frankenstein," *Studies in English Literature*, 3 (1963), pp. 461–72.
6. William Godwin, *Caleb Williams*, ed. David McCracken (London: Oxford University Press, 1970), p. 303.
7. John Locke, *An Essay Concerning Human Understanding*, ed. Alexander Campbell Fraser (Dover: New York, 1959), Vol. I, p. 130.
8. Erasmus Darwin, *Zoonomia, or the Laws of Organic Life* (Philadelphia: Edward Earle, 1818), Vol. II, p. 131.
9. Darwin, Vol. I, pp. 171–72.
10. Ralph Tymms, *Doubles in Literary Psychology* (Cambridge: Bowes and Bowes, 1949), pp. 26–27.
11. Henri F. Ellenberger, *The Discovery of the Unconscious* (New York: Basic Books, 1970), p. 128.
12. Mary Shelley uses popular Romantic images extensively, though she often transforms them to suit her own purposes. For example, the details of Frankenstein's sojourn on the lake come from Jean Jacques Rousseau, *Les Rêveries du Promeneur Solitaire* (1776–1778), which she read in 1815–1816. In the fifth prome-

nade, the "solitary walker" leaves the dinner table to take a small boat to the middle of a lake: "... *et là, m'étendant tout de mon long dans le bateau, les yeux tournés vers le ciel, je me laissais aller et dériver lentement au gré de l'eau, quelquefois pendant plusieurs heures, plongé dans mille rêveries confuses, mais délicieuses, et qui sans avoir aucun objet bien déterminé, ni constant, ne laissaient pas d'être*... ([Paris: Didier, 1948], pp. 95–96). (There, stretching myself out in the boat, with my eyes turned toward the sky, I gave up all control and let the water slowly take me where it would. Now and then during several hours, I was plunged into a thousand confused but delightful reveries which, even though having no determined or constant objective, would not leave off), (tr. by A. Wickersham.) A similar darkening of tone occurs with Mary Shelley's use of the symbol of Mont Blanc. Shelley's response to their trip up the Chamounix glacier in July of 1816 was his famous poem "Mont Blanc" in which he sees the mountain as the source of a Power that is reflected, through the Arve River, in the mind and the universe. This Power is a Platonic form, remote, abstract, and intangible. The summit is, for him, "a desert peopled by storms alone" (l. 67). Mary Shelley, however, responded to Mont Blanc quite differently. In her *History of a Six Weeks' Tour* (London: Hookham and Ollier, 1817), pp. 162–68, she describes it as a "vast animal" and a devil destined to destroy the world, citing the theories of the French naturalist Georges Buffon (1707–1788), who believed glaciers would eventually cover the earth. In *Frankenstein* the Monster lives on Mont Blanc, dwelling in the caves of ice near the summit. Thus, the Romantic image of Mont Blanc is transformed into an ominous symbol of the dangers threatening man's future.

13. Rank, pp. 85–86.
14. E. T. A. Hoffmann, *Dictungen and Schriften*, ed. W. Harich (Weinmar, 1924), Vol. VI, 65, rpt. and trans. Tymms, p. 64.
15. Carl Jung et al., *Man and His Symbols* (New York: Dell, 1972), p. 110.
16. Carl Jung, "Aion," *Psyche and Symbol*, ed. Violet S. de Laszlo (Garden City, New York: Doubleday, 1958), p. 7.
17. See Jordan M. Scher, "The Concept of the Self in Schizophrenia," in *Chronic Schizophrenia*, ed. Lawrence Appleby, Jordan Scher, and John Cumming (Glencoe, Illinois: Free Press, 1960), p. 152,

and R. D. Laing, *The Divided Self: An Existential Study in Sanity and Madness* (Baltimore: Penguin Books, 1971), p. 93.

18. "On Narcissism: An Introduction" (1914), rpt. in James Strachey et al., eds., *Standard Edition of the Complete Psychological Works of Sigmund Freud* (London: Hogarth, 1957), Vol. XIV, pp. 73–102.

19. Stanley Coleman, "The Phantom Double," *British Journal of Medical Psychology*, 14 (1934), pp. 254–73; N. Lukianowicz, "Autoscopic Phenomena," *A.M.A. Archives of Neurological Psychiatry*, 80 (1958), pp. 199–220.

20. Both references are from Michael S. Gazzaniga, *The Bisected Brain* (New York: Appleton, 1970), pp. 107, 1.

21. Shelley, *Works*, p. 271.

CHAPTER FOUR

1. Stephen Mason, *A History of the Sciences* (New York: Collier, 1962), p. 340. Mason is summarizing the beliefs of Jean Baptiste Robinet (1735–1820), Denis Diderot (1713–84), and Pierre Maupertuis (1698–1759).

2. The source for this quotation is Johann Ritter (1776–1810), who was "one of the most fascinating and typical of the Romantic scientists" according to H. A. M. Snelders, who reprints it in "Romanticism and Naturphilosophie and the Inorganic Natural Sciences 1797–1840: An Introductory Survey," *Studies in Romanticism*, 9 (1970), p. 199.

3. Mason, pp. 340, 362.

4. *The Myth of the Machine: The Pentagon of Power* (New York: Harcourt, 1970), p. 72.

5. Shelley, *Works*, p. 205.

6. *The Journals of Claire Clairmont*, ed. Marion Kingston Stocking (Cambridge: Harvard University Press, 1968), p. 34. Information on Frankenstein's castle (now a tourist attraction) can be found in Drake Douglas, *Horror!* (New York: Collier, 1969), pp. 88–89; John M. Goshko, "Frankenstein's Castle is No Horror Show," Boston *Globe*, November 19, 1972 p. B–38; Radu Florescu, *In Search of Frankenstein* (Boston: New York Graphic Society, 1975), pp. 65–95. The legend of "George of Frankenstein," a rather pallid version of the St. George tale, is retold in F. J. Kiefer, *The Legends of the Rhine from Basel to Rotterdam*, tr. L. W. Garnham (Mayence: Kapp, 1868), pp. 72–75. One of the most

exhaustive collections of Rhine folk tales has only one reference to Castle Frankenstein — as the place Charlemagne supposedly went after the death of his wife (Lewis Spence, *Heros, Tales, and Legends of the Rhine* [New York: Stokes, 1933], p. 40).

7. *Letters of P. B. Shelley*, ed. Frederick L. Jones (London: Oxford University Press, 1964), Vol. I, p. 227.

8. D. J. Palmer and R. E. Douse, "*Frankenstein*, A Moral Fable," *The Listener*, 68 (1962), p. 281.

9. Jung et. al., *Man and His Symbols*, p. 234.

10. She was surely influenced by an earlier claimant for the title, the third book of Jonathan Swift's *Gulliver's Travels* (1726), which she read in 1816. The scientists in Swift's mythical land of Laputa spend their time in abstract speculation or absurd experiments designed to help society. While they "perfect" their processes, the country falls into ruin. Marjorie Hope Nicholson, in *Voyages to the Moon* (New York: Macmillan, 1948), pp. 192–94, has shown that the experiments Swift depicts were based upon actual research done by the Royal Society, while the mechanics of the "Flying Island" of Laputa itself are a logical extension of the theories of William Gilbert on magnetism. Thus, Swift's fear of a possible nightmare for society growing out of the direction contemporary science seemed to be taking is echoed in *Frankenstein*. However, Swift's setting is imaginary and his purpose satirical; his scientists are bumbling fools and their experiments, for the most part, scatological jokes.

11. Mumford, p. 126.

12. Bloom, "*Frankenstein*, or the New Prometheus," p. 615.

CHAPTER FIVE

1. *Shelley's Prose, or the Trumpet of Prophecy*, ed. David Lee Clarke (Albuquerque: University of New Mexico Press, 1954), pp. 54–55. Some later examples of this reading are Milton Millhauser, "The Noble Savage in Mary Shelley's *Frankenstein*," *Notes and Queries*, 90 (1946), pp. 248–50; Milton Mays, "*Frankenstein*: Mary Shelley's Black Theodicy," *Southern Humanities Review*, 3 (1969), pp. 146–53; Wilfred Cude, "Mary Shelley's Modern Prometheus: A Study in the Ethics of Scientific Creativity," *Dalhousie Review*, 52 (1972), pp. 212–25; George Levine, "Frankenstein and the Tradition of Realism," *Novel*, 7 (fall 1973), pp. 14–30. The argument is neatly summed up in a sample term paper by

Anita Brooks, "Frankenstein's Lonely Monster," *Practical English Handbook*, 4th ed., (Boston: Houghton Mifflin, 1974), pp. 291–309.

2. My information on the wild man comes from Richard Bernheimer, *Wild Men in the Middle Ages* (New York: Octagon, 1970). For other possible ancestors of the Monster, see Burton Pollin, "Philosophical and Literary Sources of *Frankenstein*," *Comparative Literature*, 7 (1965), pp. 97–108; Oliver Emerson, "Legends of Cain in Old and Middle English," *PMLA*, 21 (1906), pp. 831–929; Daniel Cohen, *A Modern Look at Monsters*, (New York: Dodd, Mead, 1970). An interesting antecedent for the concept of a technological monster can be found in the "Tales, Fables, and Prophecies" of Leonardo Da Vinci; he writes of a giant from the Libyan desert who tramples men like ants — a vision, perhaps, of the monstrous potential of his military inventions (*The Notebooks of Leonardo Da Vinci*, ed. Robert Linscott [New York: Modern Library, 1957], pp. 415–17).

3. Jean Jacques Rousseau, *The Social Contract and Discourse on the Origin and Foundation of Inequality Among Mankind* (1762) (New York: Washington Square Press, 1971), p. 179.

4. Lester G. Crocker, *Jean Jacques Rousseau: The Quest (1712–1758)* (New York: Macmillan, 1968), Vol. I, 257.

5. John Milton, *Paradise Lost, Works*, Vol. II, Part One, ed. Frank Allen Patterson (New York: Columbia University Press, 1931). Book II, ll. 587–88.

6. Milton, Book II, ll. 598–600.

7. Milton, Book II, ll. 615–21.

8. Milton, Book II, ll. 624–27.

9. Milton Book II, ll. 506–11.

10. Milton, Book II, ll. 364–68.

11. Milton, Book X, ll. 743–45.

12. Milton, Book IV, ll. 86–92.

13. A point first made by M. A. Goldberg, "Moral and Myth in Mrs. Shelley's *Frankenstein*," *Keats-Shelley Journal*, 8 (1959), pp. 27–38.

CHAPTER SIX

1. The influence on *Moby Dick* and *Wuthering Heights* is discussed in Lowry Nelson, "Night Thoughts," pp. 251–53, on *Dr. Jekyll and Mr. Hyde* in Robert M. Philmus, *Into the Unknown*

(Berkeley: University of California Press, 1970), pp. 90–99, on "The Bell Tower" in John Vernon, "Melville's 'The Bell Tower'," *Studies in Short Fiction*, 7 (1970), pp. 264–76, and on science fiction in general in J. O. Bailey, *Pilgrims Through Space and Time* (New York: Argus, 1947).

2. Much of the factual information on the theatrical productions comes from Elizabeth Nitchie, "The Stage History of *Franken-stein*," *South Atlantic Quarterly*, 41 (1942), pp. 384–98, rpt. Nitchie, *Mary Shelley*, pp. 218–31.

3. My sources for inside factual information on the films are Paul Jensen, "Frankenstein," *Film Comment*, 6 (fall 1970), pp. 42–46, and Donald F. Glut, *The Frankenstein Legend* (Metuchen, N.J.: Scarecrow, 1973). Glut documents virtually every appearance of the Frankenstein story or characters in nearly every medium. Such a Herculean task in itself illustrates the ubiquitousness of the *Frankenstein* tradition; he lists in an afterward over twenty-five examples of Frankensteinia that came to his attention in the short time between finishing his manuscript and reading the proofs.

4. William Shakespeare, *Macbeth*, Act II, scene iii, lines 1–21. The situation is parallel. Fritz answers the door in the midst of Frankenstein's criminal experiments and lets in three people who will attempt to undo his blasphemy; the porter in *Macbeth* admits Macduff and Lennox soon after the murder of the king — also a crime against the natural order, committed late at night in a castle. In both cases, the interlude provides contrast and comic relief and, as Thomas De Quincey said of Shakespeare in his famous essay "On the Knocking at the Gate in *Macbeth*" (1823), makes us more aware of the unnaturalness of the crime by re-establishing the normal occurrences and rhythms of life.

5. An observation made by Roy Huss in "Almost Eve: The Creation Scene in *The Bride of Frankenstein*," *Focus on the Horror Film*, ed. Roy Huss and T. J. Ross (Englewood Cliffs, N.J.: Prentice-Hall, 1972), p. 77. I am indebted to the entire article for a shot analysis of the laboratory creation scene.

CHAPTER SEVEN

1. Frye, who has become something of a minor cult figure, was once voted one of the ten best legitimate actors on Broadway, appearing in plays as diverse as *La La Lucille* and *Six Characters in Search of an Author*. His first film success was in *Dracula*

(1931), where his cackling performance as Renfield earned him the reputation as the actor who went insane better than anyone else in pictures. Frye went on to appear in every film in the *Frankenstein* cycle through *Frankenstein Meets the Wolf Man* (1943) as either a featured performer or bit player until, on November 11, 1943, he died of a heart attack at age forty-four.

2. See Walter Evans, "Monster Movies: A Sexual Theory," *Journal of Popular Film*, 2 (1973), pp. 353–65.

3. This aspect of Monster films has been commented on before. Carlos Clarens, in *An Illustrated History of the Horror Film* (New York: Capricorn, 1968), p. 131, writes, "The monsters of the nuclear age are all creatures of the Bomb" while John Baxter, in *Science Fiction in the Cinema* (New York: Paperback Library, 1971), p. 136, states that "In all of these films it is possible to see the characteristic American ambiguity about technology... To American audiences the havoc wreaked on their homes by various dinosaurs is as welcome as the lash to a flagellant..."

4. *Civilization and Its Discontents*, tr. and ed. James Strachey (New York: Norton, 1962), pp. 69, 44.

5. Susan Sontag, in "The Imagination of Disaster," *Against Interpretation* (New York: Farrar, 1966), pp. 209–66, deals with science fiction films as fantasies of mass destruction.

6. Clarens, p. 129.

CHAPTER EIGHT

1. Erroneously of course. "Frankenstein" here is a synonym for Monster. This may have begun with Whale's *The Bride of Frankenstein*, though in that film both scientist and Monster are, after a fashion, married. *The Ghost of Frankenstein* contains an apparition of Henry Frankenstein as well as a ghostly Monster covered in dried sulfur, while in the next film the Wolf Man meets both Frankenstein's Monster and Baroness Elsa Frankenstein, making the title, *Frankenstein Meets the Wolf Man*, equally ambiguous. With *I Was a Teenage Frankenstein* such subtleties are gone; Whit Bissell's scientist could hardly pass for a teen-ager, while Gary Conway's Monster is decidedly at that awkward adolescent age.

2. Norman O. Brown, *Life Against Death* (New York: Vintage, 1959), p. 316.

A Selected Chronology of Frankenstein Films

[Dates are of American release]

s — "mad" scientist
M — Monster
a — assistant

Date	Film	Studio
1910	*Frankenstein*	Edison (USA)

1910 *Frankenstein*
DIRECTOR: J. Searle Dawley
SCREENPLAY: "from the novel"
CAST: Charles Ogle — M

Edison (USA)

1915 *Life Without Soul*
DIRECTOR: Joseph Smiley
SCREENPLAY: Jesse J. Goldburg
CAST: Percy Darrell Standing — M,
Lucy Cotton, Pauline Curley, Jack
Hopkins, George DeCarlton, William
W. Cohill — s

Ocean (USA)

1931 *Frankenstein*
DIRECTOR: James Whale
SCREENPLAY: Garrett Fort, Francis
Edwards Faragoh. Based upon the
composition of John L. Balderston.
From the novel by Mary W. Shelley.
Adapted from the play by Peggy
Webling

Universal (USA)

CAST: Colin Clive — s, Mae Clarke,
John Boles, Boris Karloff — M, Edward Van Sloan, Dwight Frye — a

1935 *The Bride of Frankenstein*   Universal (USA)
DIRECTOR: James Whale
SCREENPLAY: John L. Balderston,
William Hurlbut
CAST: Colin Clive — s, Valerie Hobson,
Ernest Thesiger — s, Brois Karloff
— M, Elsa Lanchester — M, Dwight
Frye — a

1939 *Son of Frankenstein*   Universal (USA)
DIRECTOR: Rowland V. Lee
SCREENPLAY: Willis Cooper
CAST: Basil Rathbone — s, Boris Karloff
— M, Bela Lugosi — a, Josephine
Hutchinson, Lionel Atwill

1942 *The Ghost of Frankenstein*   Universal (USA)
DIRECTOR: Erle C. Kenton
SCREENPLAY: W. Scott Darling
CAST: Sir Cedric Hardwicke — s, Lon
Chaney, Jr. — M, Lionel Atwill — s,
Bela Lugosi — a, Evelyn Ankers,
Ralph Bellamy

1943 *Frankenstein Meets the Wolf Man*   Universal (USA)
DIRECTOR: Roy William Neill
SCREENPLAY: Curt Siodmak
CAST: Patrick Knowles — s, Ilona Mas-
sey, Lon Chaney, Jr., Lionel Atwill,
Bela Lugosi — M, Maria Ouspenskaya,
Dwight Frye

1944 *House of Frankenstein*   Universal (USA)
DIRECTOR: Erle C. Kenton
SCREENPLAY: Edward T. Lowe, based
on a story by Curt Siodmak
CAST: Boris Karloff — s, Lon Chaney,
Jr., J. Carrol Naish — a, Glenn

Strange — M, Elena Verdugo, John
Carradine, Lionel Atwill

1945 *House of Dracula*   Universal (USA)
DIRECTOR: Erle C. Kenton
SCREENPLAY: Edward T. Lowe
CAST: Onslow Stevens — s, Lon Chaney,
Jr., Martha O'Driscoll, Jane Adams
— a, John Carradine, Lionel Atwill,
Skelton Knaggs, Glenn Strange — M

1948 *Abbott and Costello Meet Frankenstein*   Universal (USA)
DIRECTOR: Charles Barton
SCREENPLAY: Robert Lees, Fredric
Rinaldo, John Grant
CAST: Bud Abbott, Lou Costello, Lenore
Aubert — a, Lon Chaney, Jr., Bela
Lugosi — s, Glenn Strange — M

1957 *I Was a Teenage Frankenstein*   American-Inter-
DIRECTOR: Herbert L. Strock   national (USA)
SCREENPLAY: Kenneth Langtry
CAST: Whit Bissell — s, Phyllis Coates,
Robert Burton, Gary Conway — M,
George Lynn, John Cliff

1957 *The Curse of Frankenstein*   Hammer Films
DIRECTOR: Terence Fisher   (Great Britain)
SCREENPLAY: Jimmy Sangster
CAST: Peter Cushing — s, Christopher
Lee — M, Robert Urquhart — a,
Valerie Gaunt, Nöel Hood

1958 *Frankenstein 1970*   Allied Artists
DIRECTOR: Howard W. Koch   (USA)
SCREENPLAY: Richard Landau, George
Worthington Yates
CAST: Boris Karloff — s, Tom Duggan,
Jana Lund, Donald Barry, Mike Lane
— M, Norbert Schiller — a

1958 *The Revenge of Frankenstein*   Hammer Films
DIRECTOR: Terence Fisher   (Great Britain)

SCREENPLAY: Jimmy Sangster; additional
   dialogue by Hurford James
CAST: Peter Cushing — s, Francis Mat-
   thews — a, Eunice Grayson, Michael
   Gwynn — M, John Welsh, George
   Woodbridge, Oscar Quitak

1964 *The Evil of Frankenstein*   Hammer Films
     DIRECTOR: Freddie Francis   (Great Britain)
     SCREENPLAY: John Elder (pseud. for
       Anthony Hinds)
     CAST: Peter Cushing — s, Kiwi King-
       ston — M, Peter Woodthorpe, San-
       dor Eles — a, Duncan Lamont, Katy
       Wild, James Maxwell

1966 *Frankenstein Conquers the World*   Toho (Japan)
     DIRECTOR: Inoshiro Honda
     SCREENPLAY: Kaoru Mabuchi
     CAST: Nick Adams — m, Tadao Taka-
       shima — M, Kumi Mizuno

1966 *Frankenstein Created Woman*   Hammer/Seven
     DIRECTOR: Terence Fisher   Arts (Great
     SCREENPLAY: John Elder   Britain)
     CAST: Peter Cushing — m, Susan Den-
       berg — M, Thorley Walters, Robert
       Morris — a, M, Peter Blythe, Betty
       Warren

1969 *Frankenstein Must Be Destroyed*   Hammer Films
     DIRECTOR: Terence Fisher   (Great Britain)
     SCREENPLAY: Bert Batt
     CAST: Peter Cushing — s, Veronica
       Carlson, Simon Ward — a, Freddie
       Jones — M, Thorley Walters, Maxine
       Audley

1970 *The Horror of Frankenstein*   Hammer Films
     DIRECTOR: Jimmy Sangster   (Great Britain)
     SCREENPLAY: Jimmy Sangster, Jeremy
       Burnham

CAST: Ralph Bates — s, Dennis Price
— a, Joan Rice, Dave Prowse — M,
Graham James — a

1972 *Frankenstein and the Monster From*
Hell
DIRECTOR: Terence Fisher
SCREENPLAY: John Elder
CAST: Peter Cushing — s, Shane Briant,
Madeline Smith, Dave Prowse — M

Hammer Films
(Great Britain)

1973 *Frankenstein*
DIRECTOR: Glenn Jordan
SCREENPLAY: Sam Hall, John Landau
CAST: Robert Foxworth — s, Bo Svenson
— M, Susan Strasberg, John Karlen —
a, George Morgan — a, Robert Gentry

Dan Curtis Productions (USA)

1973 *Frankenstein: The True Story*
DIRECTOR: Jack Smight
SCREENPLAY: Christopher Isherwood,
Don Bachardy
CAST: James Mason — s, Leonard
Whiting — s, David McCallum — s,
Michael Sarrazin — M, Jane Seymour — M, Nicola Padgett, Michael
Wilding, Agnes Moorehead, Margaret Leighton, Ralph Richardson,
John Gielgud

Universal (USA)

1974 *Andy Warhol's Frankenstein*
DIRECTOR: Paul Morrissey
SCREENPLAY: Paul Morrissey
CAST: Joe Dallesandro, Monique Van
Vooren, Udo Kier — s, Arno Juerging — a, Dalila Di Lazzano — M,
Srdjan Zelenovic — M

Carlo Ponti Prod.
(USA)

1974 *Young Frankenstein*
DIRECTOR: Mel Brooks
SCREENPLAY: Gene Wilder and Mel
  Brooks
CAST: Gene Wilder — s, Peter Boyle
  — M, Marty Feldman — a, Cloris
  Leachman, Teri Garr, Kenneth Mars,
  Madeline Kahn

Twentieth Cen-
tury-Fox (USA)

A Guide to Further Reading

(The starred (*) critical works were most helpful.)

I. *Works by Mary Shelley*. There are at least ten editions of *Frankenstein* available; all are adequate. I have listed the best editions of the 1818 and 1831 versions, as well as the most interesting and accessible of her other works.

Shelley, Mary W. *Frankenstein, or The Modern Prometheus (1818).* Ed. James Rieger. New York: Bobbs-Merrill, 1974. Includes an essay "*Frankenstein* as Novel and Myth," pp. xxiv–xxxvii, and reprints entries of Byron and Polidori in the famous ghost story contest, pp. 260–87.

———. *Frankenstein, or The Modern Prometheus* (1831). Ed. M. K. Joseph. London: Oxford University Press, 1969.

———. *Mathilda.* Ed. Elizabeth Nitchie. Chapel Hill: University of North Carolina Press, 1959.

———. *The Last Man.* Ed. Hugh J. Luke, Jr. Lincoln: University of Nebraska Press, 1965.

———. *Letters.* Ed. Frederick L. Jones. Norman: University of Oklahoma Press, 1946.

———. *Journal.* Ed. Frederick L. Jones. Norman: University of Oklahoma Press, 1947.

II. *Biographies of Mary Shelley*.

Bigland, Eileen. *Mary Shelley.* London: Cassell & Company, 1959.

Church, Richard. *Mary Shelley (1797–1851).* New York: Viking, 1928.

Gerson, Noel B. *Daughter of Earth and Water: A Biography of Mary Wollstonecraft Shelley.* New York: William Morrow, 1973.

Grylls, R. Glynn. *Mary Shelley.* London: Oxford University Press, 1938.

Kmetz, Gail. "Mary Shelley: In the Shadow of *Frankenstein.*" *Ms.*, February 15, 1975, pp. 12–16.

Leighton, Margaret. *Shelley's Mary: A Life of Mary Wollstonecraft Shelley.* New York: Farrar, Straus, and Giroux, 1973.

Marshall, Mrs. Julian. *The Life and Letters of Mary Wollstonecraft Shelley.* 2 vols. London: Richard Bentley & Sons, 1889.

*Nitchie, Elizabeth. *Mary Shelley: Author of "Frankenstein."* New Brunswick, N.J.: Rutgers University Press, 1953. Rpt. Westport, Connecticut: Greenwood, 1970.

*Norman, Sylva. "Mary Wollstonecraft Shelley." *Shelley and His Circle*, III. Ed. Kenneth Neill Cameron. Cambridge Mass.: Harvard University Press, 1970, pp. 397–422.

*Spark, Muriel. *Child of Light: A Reassessment of Mary Wollstone-craft Shelley.* Hadleigh, Essex: Tower Bridge, 1951. Includes criticism of the major novels and an abridgement of *The Last Man.*

*Walling, William. *Mary Shelley.* New York: Twayne, 1972. Incorporates much excellent biographical material in an extensive study of Mary Shelley's writings.

III. *Criticism of Frankenstein.*

*Bloom, Harold. "*Frankenstein,* or the New Prometheus." *Partisan Review*, 32 (1965), pp. 611–18. Rpt. in *Ringers in the Tower.* Chicago: University of Chicago Press, 1971, pp. 119–29. Also rpt. as the afterward to *Frankenstein.* New York: Signet, 1965, pp. 212–23. Discusses *Frankenstein* in light of the Romantic mythology of the self.

Brooks, Anita. "Frankenstein's Lonely Monster." *Practical English Handbook*, 4th ed. Eds. Floyd Watkins, William Dillingham, Edwin Martin. Boston: Houghton Mifflin, 1974, pp. 287–308.

Callahan, Patrick J. "*Frankenstein,* Bacon and the 'Two Truths.' " *Extrapolation*, 14 (December 1972), pp. 39–48. Argues that the novel refutes Bacon's Enlightenment view of science — that all research will ultimately work for the good of man.

Crafts, Stephen. "*Frankenstein:* Camp Curiosity or Premonition?" *Catalyst*, 3 (1968), pp. 96–103. An unlikely characterization of the Monster as a Marcusean "one-dimensional man."

*Cude, Wilfred. "Mary Shelley's Modern Prometheus: A Study in the Ethics of Scientific Creativity." *Dalhousie Review*, 52 (1972), pp. 212–25.

A Guide to Further Reading

*Fleck, P. D. "Mary Shelley's Notes to Shelley's Poems and *Frankenstein.*" *Studies in Romanticism,* 6 (1967), pp. 226–54.

Florescu, Radu. *In Search of Frankenstein.* New York: New York Graphic Society, 1975. A personal narrative that visits the places behind the novel and briefly surveys its career in print, on stage, and on film.

*Goldberg, M. A. "Moral and Myth in Mrs. Shelley's *Frankenstein.*" *Keats-Shelley Journal,* 8 (1959), pp. 27–38. Examines Frankenstein's tale as a moral exemplum given to Robert Walton.

*Levine, George. "*Frankenstein* and the Tradition of Realism." *Novel,* 7 (fall 1973), pp. 14–30. The novel as an early example of attitudes and techniques that were to become central to the realist tradition.

Lund, Mary G. "Mary Godwin Shelley and the Monster." *University of Kansas City Review,* 27 (1962), pp. 253–58. A brief look at some autobiographical aspects of *Frankenstein.*

McKinney, John. "Nietzche and the *Frankenstein* Creature." *Dalhousie Review,* 41 (1962), pp. 40–48.

Mays, Milton A. "*Frankenstein:* Mary Shelley's Black Theodicy." *Southern Humanities Review,* 3 (1969), pp. 146–53.

Millhauser, Milton. "The Noble Savage in Mary Shelley's *Frankenstein.*" *Notes and Queries,* 190 (1946), pp. 248–50.

*Moers, Ellen. "Female Gothic: The Monster's Mother." *New York Review of Books,* 21 (March 21, 1974), pp. 24–28.

Palmer, D. J., and Douse, R. E. "*Frankenstein:* A Moral Fable." *The Listener,* 68 (1962), pp. 281–84.

*Pollin, Burton R. "Philosophical and Literary Sources of *Frankenstein.*" *Comparative Literature,* 17 (1965), pp. 97–108.

Prescott, F. C. "*Wieland* and *Frankenstein.*" *American Literature,* 2 (1930), pp. 172–73.

*Rieger, James. "Dr. Polidori and the Genesis of *Frankenstein.*" *Studies in English Literature,* 3 (1963), pp. 461–72. Rpt. in *The Mutiny Within: The Heresies of Percy Bysshe Shelley.* New York: Braziller, 1967, p. 237.

*Rosenberg, Samuel. "*Frankenstein* or Daddy's Little Monster." *Confessions of a Trivialist.* Baltimore: Penguin, 1972.

Small, Christopher. *Mary Shelley's "Frankenstein": Tracing the Myth.* Pittsburgh: University of Pittsburgh Press, 1973. Pub. in England as *Ariel Like a Harpy: Shelley, Mary, and "Frankenstein."* London: Victor Gollancz, Ltd., 1972. Strongly emphasizes the relationship of Godwin and Shelley to Mary Shelley's novel.

*Swingle, L. J. "Frankenstein's Monster and Its Romantic Relatives; Problems of Knowledge in English Romanticism." *Texas Studies in Literature and Language*, 15 (1973), pp. 51–66. The Monster as one of a family of "Strangers" found in Romantic poetry — a being whose essential nature is unknowable.

Wade, Philip Tyree. "Frankenstein." Influence and Intent in the Prose Fiction of Percy and Mary Shelley." Diss. University of Carolina at Chapel Hill, 1966, pp. 70–123. Calls the novel an awkward conglomeration, "vivified by the spark of Shelley's influence."

IV. *Criticism of Plays, Films, and Literature Influenced by Frankenstein.*

Ackerman, Forrest J., ed. *The Frankenscience Monster.* New York: Ace, 1969. An uneven collection of essays and reminiscences written to commemorate Boris Karloff's death.

Aldiss, Brian W. *The Billion Year Spree: The True History of Science Fiction.* Garden City, N.Y.: Doubleday, 1973. Examines *Frankenstein* as one of the early steps in the development of science fiction, pp. 20–30.

Amis, Kingsley. "Dracula, Frankenstein, Sons & Co." *What Became of Jane Austen? And Other Questions.* New York: Harcourt Brace Jovanovich, 1970, pp. 125–35.

———. *New Maps of Hell: A Survey of Science Fiction.* New York: Harcourt Brace Jovanovich, 1960. Mentions *Frankenstein*, pp. 32–33.

Annan, David. *Movie Fantastic: Beyond the Dream Machine.* Thetford, Norwalk, Conn.: Bounty, 1974. Looks at dream images in horror and science fiction films, including the Universal Frankensteins, pp. 14, 32–34.

Aylesworth, Thomas G. *Monsters from the Movies.* Philadelphia: Lippincott, 1972. The tradition of man-made monsters, including the Golem, is discussed, pp. 22–45.

Bailey, J. O. *Pilgrims Through Space and Time: Trends and Patterns in Scientific and Utopian Fiction.* New York: Argus, 1947. Rpt. Westport, Conn.: Greenwood, 1972. In the index, p. 339, Bailey lists ten references to *Frankenstein*; in the text, he examines numerous short stories on the theme scattered through the reams of magazine science fiction published in the thirties and forties.

A Guide to Further Reading

*Baxter, John. *Science Fiction in the Cinema*. New York: Paperback Library, 1970.

Beck, Calvin Thomas. *Heros of the Horrors*. New York: Collier, 1975.

Brustein, Robert. "Reflections on Horror Movies," Partisan Review, 25 (1958), pp. 288–96.

Butler, Ivan. *Horror in the Cinema*. New York: Paperback Library, 1971.

*Clarens, Carlos. *An Illustrated History of the Horror Film*. New York: Capricorn, 1968.

De Camp, L. Sprague. *Science-Fiction Handbook: The Writing of Imaginative Literature*. New York: Hermitage House, 1953.

Diehl, Digby. "Mel Brooks." *Action*, 10 (January–February 1975), pp. 18–21. Brooks interviewed on the set of *Young Frankenstein.*

Douglas, Drake. *Horror!* New York: Collier, 1969. Contains a dramatized history of "The Monster," pp. 77–129.

Durgnat, Raymond. *A Mirror for England: British Movies from Austerity to Affluence*. London: Faber & Faber, 1970. Discusses Hammer horror films, pp. 218–28.

*Evans, Walter. "Monster Movies: A Sexual Theory." *Journal of Popular Film*, 2 (1973), pp. 353–65.

Everson, William K. "Horror Films." *Films in Review*, 5 (1954), pp. 12–23.

Gifford, Denis. *Movie Monsters*. New York: Dutton, 1969. Contains a chapter, "Creation," which discusses the Monster and the Golem, pp. 9–45.

———. *A Pictorial History of Horror Movies*. London: Hamlyn, 1973.

*Glut, Donald F. *The Frankenstein Legend: A Tribute to Mary Shelley and Boris Karloff*. Metuchen, N.J.: Scarecrow, 1973. An exhaustive survey.

*Hitchens, Gordon. " 'A Breathless Eagerness in the Audience...' Historical Notes on Dr. Frankenstein and His Monster." *Film Comment*, 6 (spring 1970), pp. 49–51. Popular reaction to the early stage plays.

*Huss, Roy, and Ross, T. J., eds. *Focus on the Horror Film*. Englewood Cliffs, N.J.: Prentice-Hall, 1972. An excellent collection of essays that includes Roy Huss, "Almost Eve: The Creation Scene in *The Bride of Frankenstein*," pp. 74–82.

*Jensen, Paul. "On *Frankenstein*." *Film Comment*, 6 (fall 1970), pp. 42–46. A knowledgeable analysis of the 1931 film.

*Johnson, William, ed. *Focus on the Science Fiction Film*. Englewood Cliffs, N.J.: Prentice-Hall, 1972. Provides a useful survey of the genre through a collection of essays and mentions the influence of *Frankenstein*, pp. 6, 11, 108.

Kane, Joe. "Beauties, Beasts, and Male Chauvinist Monsters: The Plight of Women in the Horror Film." *Take One*, 4 (March–April 1973), pp. 8–10. A sketchy treatment of the theme; mentions Mary Shelley and *Frankenstein*.

*Miyoshi, Masao. *The Divided Self: A Perspective on the Literature of the Victorians*. New York: New York University Press, 1969. Discusses *Frankenstein* as part of a literary tradition of "self-division," pp. 79–89.

Moskowitz, Sam. *Explorers of the Infinite: Shapers of Science Fiction*. Cleveland: World, 1963. Contains a chapter, "The Sons of Frankenstein," pp. 33–45, which briefly traces the development of the myth.

Moss, Robert F. *Karloff and Company: The Horror Film*. New York: Pyramid, 1974.

Neff, Renfreu. *The Living Theatre: USA*. New York: Bobbs-Merrill, 1970.

*Nelson, Lowry, Jr. "Night Thoughts on the Gothic Novel." *Yale Review*, 52 (1962), pp. 236–57.

*Nitchie, Elizabeth. "The Stage History of *Frankenstein*." *South Atlantic Quarterly*, 41 (1942), pp. 384–398. Rpt. in *Mary Shelley: Author of "Frankenstein,"* pp. 218–31.

*Philmus, Robert M. *Into the Unknown: The Evolution of Science Fiction from Francis Godwin to H. G. Wells*. Berkeley: University of California Press, 1970. Discusses *Frankenstein* as part of the Faustian theme in science fiction, pp. 82–90.

*Pirie, David. *A Heritage of Horror: The English Gothic Cinema, 1946–1972*. New York: Avon, 1973. Links the Hammer horror films to the English Gothic tradition and includes a chapter, "Approaches to Frankenstein: Fisher, Francis, and Sangster," pp. 66–81.

*Ringel, Harry. "The Horrible Hammer Films of Terence Fisher." *Take One*, 3 (January–February 1972), pp. 8–12. A short, intelligent discussion.

Rostagno, Aldo, with Beck, Julian, and Malina, Judith. *We, The Living Theatre*. New York: Ballantine, 1970. Contains many pictures from the Living Theater production of *Frankenstein*.

*Sontag, Susan. "The Imagination of Disaster." *Against Interpretation.* New York: Farrar, Straus & Giroux, 1966, p. 209.

Steinbrunner, Chris and Goldblatt, Burt. *Cinema of the Fantastic.* New York: Saturday Review Press, 1972. Includes summary and stills from *The Bride of Frankenstein*, pp. 89–106.

Vernon, John. "Melville's 'The Bell Tower.'" *Studies in Short Fiction*, 7 (1970), pp. 264–76.

Wharton, Lawrence. "*Godzilla to Latitude Zero: The Cycle of the Technological Monster.*" *Journal of Popular Film*, 3 (1974), pp. 31–38. Sees the Japanese cycle of monster films portraying the gradual acceptance of technology by mankind.

V. *Related Materials.*

Aldiss, Brian W. *Frankenstein Unbound.* New York: Random House, 1974. A time travel novel that links Mary Shelley to a "real" Frankenstein.

Anobile, Richard J., ed. *Frankenstein.* New York: Avon, 1974. Recreates the 1931 film.

Bernheimer, Richard. *Wild Men in the Middle Ages.* New York: Octagon, 1970.

Broege, Valerie. "Views of Technology in Classical Mythology and Modern Literature." *Classical News and Views*, 17 (April 1973), pp. 37–51.

Brown, Norman O. *Life Against Death: The Psychoanalytical Meaning of History.* New York: Vintage, 1959.

Clairmont, Claire. *Journals.* Ed. Marion Kingston Stocking. Cambridge, Mass.: Harvard University Press, 1968.

Cohen, Daniel. *A Modern Look at Monsters.* New York: Dodd, Mead, 1970.

Coleman, Stanley. "The Phantom Double." *British Journal of Medical Psychology*, 14 (1934), pp. 254–73. Discusses Capgras' syndrome, and belief in doubles among the Aranda tribes of Central Australia.

Coleridge, Samuel T. *Collected Letters.* Ed. Earl Leslie Griggs, 6 vol. London: Oxford University Press, 1956–1971.

Crawley, A. E. "Doubles." *Encyclopedia of Religion and Ethics.* Ed. James Hastings. New York: Scribners, 1912. Vol. IV, pp. 853–60.

Crocker, Lester G. *Jean-Jacques Rousseau: The Quest (1712–1758).* New York: Macmillan, 1968.

Darwin, Erasmus. *Zoonomia, or the Laws of Organic Life.* 2 vol. Philadelphia: Edward Earle, 1818.

Da Vinci, Leonardo. *Notebooks.* Ed. Robert Linscott. New York: Modern Library, 1957.

Douglas, Mary. "The Abominations of Leviticus." *Purity and Danger: An Analysis of the Concepts of Pollution and Taboo.* New York: Praeger, 1966, p. 41. "The abominable" examined by a structural anthropologist.

Downey, J. E. "Literary Self-Projection." *Psychological Review,* 19 (1912), pp. 299–311.

Ellenberger, Henri F. *The Discovery of the Unconscious: The History and Evolution of Dynamic Psychiatry.* New York: Basic Books, 1970.

Emerson, Oliver. "Legends of Cain in Old and Middle English." *PMLA,* 21 (1906), pp. 831–929. Includes a list of references to monsters in Middle English poetry.

Field, Edward. *Variety Photoplays.* New York: Grove, 1967. Poems, including, in a section entitled "Old Movies," "Frankenstein" (p. 13), "The Bride of Frankenstein" (p. 22), and "The Return of Frankenstein" (p. 39).

Freud, Sigmund. "On Narcissism: An Introduction." *Standard Edition of the Complete Psychological Works.* Tr. and ed. James Strachey, et al. 23 vols. London: Hogarth, 1957, Vol. XIV, pp. 73–102.

———. *Civilization and Its Discontents.* Tr. and Ed. James Strachey. New York: Norton, 1962.

Gaylen, Willard. "The *Frankenstein* Myth Becomes a Reality — We Have the Awful Knowledge to Make Exact Copies of Human Beings." *The New York Times Magazine,* March 5, 1972, pp. 12–13, 41–44, 48–49.

Gazzaniga, Michael S. *The Bisected Brain.* New York: Appleton-Century-Crofts, 1970.

Godwin, William. *Caleb Williams.* Ed. David McCracken. London: Oxford University Press, 1970.

———. *The Elopement of Percy Bysshe Shelley and Mary Wollstonecraft Godwin.* With Commentary by H. Buxton Forman, L. B. The Bibliophile Society, 1911.

Goshko, John M. "Frankenstein's Castle Is No Horror Show." Boston *Globe,* November 19, 1972, p. B-38, cols. 1–5.

Hadfield, J. A. *Dreams and Nightmares.* Baltimore: Penguin, 1954.

A Guide to Further Reading

Hall, Sam, and Landau, Richard. *Frankenstein* (unpub. script). Los Angeles: Dan Curtis Productions, 1973.

Holcolm, Adele M. "John Sell Cotman's *Dismasted Brig* and the Motif of the Drifting Boat." *Studies in Romanticism*, 14 (winter 1975), pp. 29–40. A study of the image in Romantic art and poetry.

Isherwood, Christopher, and Bachardy, Don. *Frankenstein: The True Story*. New York: Avon, 1973.

Jung, Carl G., et al. *Man and His Symbols*. New York: Dell, 1972.

———. *Psyche and Symbol*. Ed. Violet S. de Lazlo. Garden City, N.J.: Doubleday, 1958.

Kiefer, F. J. *The Legends of the Rhine from Basel to Rotterdam*. Tr. L. W. Garnham. Mayence: David Kapp, 1868. Contains the legend "George of Frankenstein," pp. 72–75.

Laing, R. D. *The Divided Self: An Existential Study of Sanity and Madness*. Baltimore: Penguin, 1971.

Lee, Walt. *Reference Guide to Fantastic Films: Science Fiction, Fantasy & Horror*. 3 vol. Los Angeles: Chelsea-lee Books, 1972–1974.

Locke, John. *An Essay Concerning Human Understanding*. Ed. Alexander Campbell Fraser. 2 vols. New York: Dover, 1959.

Lovell, Ernest J., Jr. "Byron and the Byronic Hero in the Novels of Mary Shelley." *Studies in English (University of Texas)*, 30 (1951), pp. 158–83.

Lukianowicz, N. "Autoscopic Phenomena." *A.M.A. Archives of Neurological Psychiatry*, 80 (1958), pp. 199–220.

Luke, Hugh. "*The Last Man*: Mary Shelley's Myth of the Solitary." *Prairie Schooner*, 39 (1965), pp. 316–27.

Mack, John E. *Nightmares and Human Conflict*. Boston: Houghton Mifflin, 1974.

Mason, Stephen F. *A History of the Sciences*. New York: Collier, 1962.

Milner, H. M. *Frankenstein, or the Man and the Monster!* London: John Duncombe, 1823.

Milton, John. *Paradise Lost. Works*, Vol II, Part One. Ed. Frank Allen Patterson, New York: Columbia University Press, 1931.

Mumford, Lewis. *The Myth of the Machine: The Pentagon of Power*. New York: Harcourt, Brace and World, 1966.

Murray, Henry. "The Possible Nature of a 'Mythology' to Come." *Myth and Mythmaking*. Ed. Henry Murray. New York: George Braziller, 1960.

Nicholson, Marjorie Hope. *Voyages to the Moon.* New York: Macmillan, 1948.

Peck, W. E. "The Biographical Element in the Novels of Mary Wollstonecraft Shelley." *PMLA,* 38 (1923), pp. 196–219.

Pollin, Burton R. "Mary Shelley as the Parvenue." *Review of English Literature (Leeds),* 8 (1967), pp. 9–21.

Praz, Mario. *The Romantic Agony.* Tr. Angus Davidson with introd. Frank Kermode. London: Oxford University Press, 1970.

Rank, Otto. *The Double: A Psychoanalytic Study.* Tr. and ed. Harry Tucker, Jr. Chapel Hill: University of North Carolina Press, 1971.

Rousseau, Jean-Jacques. *The Social Contract and Discourse on the Origin and Foundation of Inequality Among Mankind.* New York: Washington Square Press, 1971.

———. *Les Reveries Du Promeneur Solitaire.* Ed. John S. Spink. Paris: Librairie Marcel Didier, 1948.

Saagpakk, Paul F. "A Survey of Psychopathology in British Literature from Shakespeare to Hardy." *Literature and Psychology,* 18 (1968), pp. 135–65. Discusses, among other things, the Gothic novel and the poetry of Byron.

Scher, Jordan. "The Concept of the Self in Schizophrenia." *Chronic Schizophrenia.* Ed. Lawrence Appleby et al. Glencoe, Ill.: Free Press, 1960.

Shelley, Mary W. *History of a Six Weeks' Tour Through Part of France, Switzerland, Germany, and Holland, with letters descriptive of a sail round the lake of Geneva and of the glaciers of Chamouni.* London: T. Hookham, jun. and C. and T. Ollier, 1817.

———. *Frankenstein, or The Modern Prometheus.* 3 vol. London: Lackington, Hughes, Harding, Mavor, and Jones, 1818 (first edition).

Shelley, Percy B. *Complete Poetical Works.* Ed. Thomas Hutchinson. London: Oxford University Press, 1961.

———. *Shelley's Prose or The Trumpet of Prophecy.* Ed. David Lee Clark. Albuquerque: University of New Mexico Press, 1954.

———. *Letters.* Ed. Frederick L. Jones. 2 vols. London: Oxford University Press, 1964.

Snelders, H. A. M. "Romanticism and Naturphilosophie and the Inorganic Natural Sciences 1797–1840: An Introductory Survey." *Studies in Romanticism,* 9 (1970), pp. 193–215.

Spence, Lewis. *Heroes, Tales, and Legends of the Rhine.* New York: Frederick Stokes, 1933.

A Guide to Further Reading

Trelawny, Edward John. *Letters.* Ed. H. Buxton Forman. London: Oxford University Press, 1910. Rpt. New York: Amis, 1973.
Tymms, Ralph. *Doubles in Literary Psychology.* Cambridge: Bowes and Bowes, 1949.
Whitehead, Alfred North. *Science and the Modern World.* New York: Macmillan, 1967.

Index

Abbott and Costello Meet Frankenstein, 116
"Alastor" (P. B. Shelley), 38
Alchemy and magic, 55–63
Aldini, Giovanni, 53
Androids. *See* Robots and androids
Andy Warhol's Frankenstein, 139–42, 150, 155
Aquinas, Thomas, 56
Atwill, Lionel, 108–12, 114
"Automatons" (Hoffmann), 53

Bachardy, Don, 134
Balderston, John, 87
Beast From 20,000 Fathoms, The, 117
Beckford, William, 57
Bellamy, Ralph, 111
"Bell Tower, The" (Melville), 84, 173n
Beowulf, 9, 68
Blake, William, 38, 68, 79
Blumenbach, Johann Friedrich, 54
Borderers, The (Wordsworth), 38

Boyle, Peter, 149
Bride of Frankenstein, The, 84, 97–105, 107, 127, 137, 155, 174n
Brontë, Emily, 84, 172n
Brooks, Mel, 2, 133, 149, 150, 155. *See also Young Frankenstein*
Brown, Charles Brockden, 37, 39
Brown, Norman O., 122
Byron, George Gordon, Lord, 79; *Childe Harold's Pilgrimage*, 38; and *Frankenstein*, 3, 13, 16–17, 35, 52; portrayed in films, 97, 134

Cabinet of Dr. Caligari, The, 87
Caleb Williams (Godwin), 37–38
Castle, The (Kafka), 8
Chaney, Lon, Jr., 106, 111, 116
Childe Harold's Pilgrimage (Byron), 38
Christabel (Coleridge), 38
Clairmont, Claire, 12–13, 34, 39, 58
Clairmont, Mary Jane (Mrs. William Godwin), 11
Clarke, May, 68

Clive, Colin, 86, 88, 93, 96–97, 110, 149
Coleridge, Samuel T., 16, 38, 166n
Colman, Stanley, 49
Colossus: The Forbin Project, 119
Cooke, Thomas P., 85
Cooper, Willis, 108
Curse of Frankenstein, The, 125–27, 130, 136, 144
Cushing, Peter, 125–31, 134, 137, 140

Dante Alighieri, 9, 81, 83
Darwin, Erasmus, 39–40, 52
Denberg, Susan, 128
Dippel, Johann K., 58
Divine Comedy, The (Dante), 9, 81, 83
Dr. Strangelove, 2, 119
Doppelgänger. *See* Doubles
Dostoevski, Feodor M., 38
Double, The (Dostoevski), 38
Doubles: in films, 86, 96; in *Frankenstein,* 8, 40–47, 50–51, 67, 165–66n; pattern of tales, 37–38, 43; recent study of, 47–50, 64; Romantic interest in, 38–40, 66; and technology, 52–53, 63–65, 81
Dracula (film), 86
Dreams: *Frankenstein* and, 19–33; monsters in, 31; myth and, 1; and Mary Shelley, 3–4, 9, 12, 41; and P. B. Shelley, 39; and Claire Clairmont, 39

Edgar Huntly (Brown), 37, 39
"Epipsychidion" (P. B. Shelley), 38

Essay Concerning Human Understanding, An (Locke), 38–39
Evil of Frankenstein, The, 129

Faust (Goethe), 56. *See also Frankenstein, or the Modern Prometheus*
Film, 1–3, 85–86, 143. *See also individual titles*
Fisher, Terence, 125, 129, 130
Fleetwood (Godwin), 37
Florey, Robert, 88–89
Forbidden Planet, 119–22
Foxworth, Robert, 144
Frankenstein (1910 film), 86
Frankenstein (1931 film), 84–97, 106–7, 143–44, 147, 151
Frankenstein (1973 teleplay), 143–49
Frankenstein (Living Theatre production), 2
Frankenstein Created Woman, 128, 130
Frankenstein De Sade, 1
Frankenstein Meets the Wolf Man, 106, 110, 112–13, 174n
Frankenstein Must Be Destroyed, 128, 130–31
Frankenstein 1970, 124
Frankenstein, or the Man and the Monster! (Milner), 84
Frankenstein, or the Modern Prometheus (M. Shelley), 4; alchemy and, 55, 59–62; doubles and, 40–47, 165–66n; dreams and, 3–4, 9, 19–33; Faustian theme and, 56–58, 64; Gothicism and, 35–37; Monster in, 66–82, mythic patterns in, 8–9; narrative frame of, 15–18, 82–83; plot summary

of, 5–7; Promethean theme in, 56–57, 83, 89; reflected directly in films, 1–3, 88, 96, 99–100, 103, 116–120, 132–36, 143, 147, 149; and science fiction, 64–65, 165n. *See also* Shelley, Mary W.

Freud, Sigmund, 48, 118

Frye, Dwight, 87, 90–91, 101, 107, 111, 113, 173–74n

Galvani, Luigi, 53, 65

Gaylen, Willard, 65

Ghost of Frankenstein, The, 106, 110–12, 116, 174n

Gielgud, Sir John, 134

Gilgamesh, 9, 68

Godwin, Mary W. *See* Shelley, Mary W.

Godwin, William: as father, 11–13, 166n; in *Frankenstein,* 18, 33; and P. B. Shelley, 59; works: *Caleb Williams,* 37–38; *Fleetwood,* 37; *St. Leon,* 37, 55

Goethe, Johann Wolfgang von, 56, 75

Golem, The, 87–88, 111

Gosse, William, 87

Gothic literature, 35–37, 39, 51, 57, 87, 129, 131. *See also* Doubles

Gulliver's Travels (Swift), 171n

Hall, Charles D., 87

Hall, Mordaunt, 97

Hall, Sam, 143

Hammer Films. *See* A Selected Chronology of Frankenstein Films

Hardwicke, Sir Cedric, 111

Hawks, Howard, 117

History of a Six Weeks' Tour (M. Shelley), 169n

Hitler, Adolf, 99, 104–5

Hobson, Valerie, 97

Hoffmann, E. T. A., 43, 53

House of Dracula, 106, 110, 114–16

House of Frankenstein, 106, 113–14, 123

Hume, Cyril, 119

Hunchback of Notre Dame, The (1923), 90

Hunchback of Notre Dame, The (1939), 114

Hurlbut, William, 87

Invisible Agent, The, 107

Isherwood, Christopher, 134

I Was a Teenage Frankenstein, 123–24, 174n

I Was a Teenage Werewolf, 123

Jaquet-Droz, Pierre and Henri, 53–54

Jesse James Meets Frankenstein's Daughter, 1

Journey's End (Sherriff), 88

Jung, Carl G., 48, 66

Kafka, Franz, 8

Karloff, Boris: as the Monster in *Frankenstein* (1931), 86, 88, 91–93, 95–96, 147; in *The Bride of Frankenstein,* 97–103, 106; in *Son of Frankenstein,* 108–109; performance recalled in later films, 126, 146–48, 155; as the scientist, 113, 124

Kempelen, Baron Wolfgang, 54

Kenton, Erle C., 114

Kier, Udo, 140
King Kong, 100, 152
Knaggs, Skelton, 114

Laing, R. D., 48
Lanchester, Elsa, 97, 155
Landau, Richard, 143
Lee, Christopher, 125–26
Levi-Strauss, Claude, 132
Lewis, Matthew G., 57, 129
Life Without Soul, 86
Lives (Plutarch), 75
Living Theatre, 2
Locke, John, 38–39
Lugosi, Bela, 88, 106, 108, 112, 116
Lukianowicz, N., 49

Macbeth (Shakespeare), 90, 173n
Magnus, Albertus, 55–56, 59
Mason, James, 133–34
Mathilda (M. Shelley), 167n
Meckel, Johann Friedrich, 54
Melville, Herman, 84, 173n
Mesmer, Franz Anton, 40
Milner, H. M., 84
Milton, John. *See Paradise Lost*
Milton (Blake), 38
Moby Dick (Melville), 84, 172n
Monk, The (Lewis), 57, 129
Monsters. *See* Myth
"Mont Blanc" (P. B. Shelley), 169n
Morrissey, Paul, 133, 139–41, 150, 155
Mumford, Lewis, 54
Murray, Henry A., 11
Myth: creators of, 11; and dreams, 1; and film, 1–3, 85–86; and monsters, 67–68, 118, 172n, 174n; patterns of, 8–9, 83, 132. *See*
also *Frankenstein, or the Modern Prometheus*

Nightmare. *See* Dreams
Nyby, Christian, 117

Ogle, Charles, 86
Ouspenskaya, Maria, 107

Paracelsus, Philippus, A., 55–56, 59
Paradise Lost (Milton), 68–81
Parker, Edwin, 106
"Parvenue, The" (M. Shelley), 167n
Payne, John Howard, 14
Paz, Octavio, 132
Peake, Richard Brinsley, 85
Plutarch, 75
Poe, Edgar Allen, 38
Polidori, John W., 3, 35, 38, 134
Pratt, William Henry. *See* Karloff, Boris
Praz, Mario, 34–35
Presumption, or the Fate of Frankenstein (Peake), 85, 90
Pretorious, Dr. *See* Thesiger, Ernest
Price, James, 58
Prometheus, 56–57, 83, 89
Prometheus Bound (P. B. Shelley), 50–51, 56–57
Psychology: and doubles, 38–40, 48–49, 66; and Mary Shelley, 13–15, 31–33; and *Frankenstein*, 15–31, 40–47, 165–66n

Radcliffe, Mrs. Ann, 129
Rank, Otto, 43, 48
Rathbone, Basil, 108–9, 149

Index

Rebel Without a Cause, 124
Return of the Vampire, The, 107
Revenge of Frankenstein, The, 127–28, 130, 134–35
Rêveries du Promeneur Solitaire, Les (Rousseau), 168–69n
Richardson, Sir Ralph, 134
Rime of the Ancient Mariner, The (Coleridge), 16
Robots and androids, 2, 53–54, 56, 58, 64–65
Rousseau, Jean-Jacques, 71–72, 168–69n

Saint-Germain, Comte, 59
St. Irvyne (P. B. Shelley), 38
St. Leon (Godwin), 37, 55
"Sandman, The" (Hoffmann), 43, 53
Science and technology: criticism of, 54–55, 62–65, 69, 122, 131, 171n; and film, 86, 143; and the Industrial Revolution, 79, 83; and monsters, 81, 117–18, 174n; Romantic theories of, 53–54. *See also* Doubles
Shakespeare, William, 90, 119, 173n
Shelley, Harriet, 13
Shelley, Mary W.: childhood, 11–13, 16, 166n; creation of *Frankenstein*, 3–4, 9, 12, 34–37, 41; *History of a Six Weeks' Tour*, 169n; *Mathilda*, 166–67n; opinions, 34–35, 50–53; "Parvenue, The," 166–67n; personality, 13–19, 31–33; portrayed in films, 97, 134; and the Shelley circle, 3, 12–17, 52–53. *See also Franken-*

stein, or the Modern Prometheus
Shelley, Percy B.: and doubles, 39; and dreams, 39; and Mary, 3, 12–13, 16; interest in science and alchemy, 52, 55, 59; opinion of *Frankenstein*, 35, 67; portrayed on film, 97, 134; portrayed in *Frankenstein*, 16–17, 59, 167–68n; works: "Alastor," 38; "Epipsychidion," 38; "Mont Blanc," 169n; *Prometheus Unbound*, 50–51, 56–57; *St. Irvyne*, 38
Sherriff, R. C., 88
Smith, Richard John ("O."), 85
Son of Dracula, 108
Son of Frankenstein, 106, 108–111, 154
Sorcerer, The (Weber), 57
Sorrows of Werther, The (Goethe), 75
Standing, Percy Darrell, 86
Stevenson, Robert Louis, 38, 84, 172–73n
Strange, Glenn, 106
Strange Case of Dr. Jekyll and Mr. Hyde, The (Stevenson), 38, 84, 172–73n
Strickfaden, Kenneth, 89, 151
Swift, Jonathan, 171n

Technology. *See* Science and technology
Tempest, The (Shakespeare), 119
Thesiger, Ernest (as Dr. Pretorious), 98–99, 101–104, 123, 137
Thing, The, 117–18
Trelawney, Edward J., 14, 34

Tuttle, William, 149
2001 — A Space Odyssey, 119

Universal films. *See* A Selected Chronology of Frankenstein Films

Van Sloan, Edward, 86–87
Vathek (Beckford), 57
Vaucanson, Jacques de, 54

Wade, Philip, 35
Wald, George, 64
Weber, Veit, 57
Webling, Peggy, 87
Wegener, Paul, 87, 111
Weine, Robert, 87

Whale, James: and *Frankenstein* (1931), 86, 88–89, 93–97, 116–117; and *The Bride of Frankenstein*, 97–98, 100–101, 105-7, 120–21; techniques compared to later films, 128–29, 144, 150
Wieland (Brown), 37
"William Wilson" (Poe), 38
Wolfe, Bud, 106
Wollstonecraft, Mary, 11, 32
Wordsworth, William, 38
Wuthering Heights (Brontë), 84, 172n

Young Frankenstein, 2, 149–55

Zoonomia (Darwin), 39–40